TULLOH ON RUNNING

TULLOH ON RUNNING

Bruce Tulloh

HEINEMANN : LONDON

William Heinemann Ltd

LONDON MELBOURNE TORONTO

CAPE TOWN AUCKLAND

© Bruce Tulloh, 1968

First Published 1968

434 79750 2

MADE AND PRINTED IN GREAT BRITAIN BY
MORRISON AND GIBB LIMITED, LONDON AND EDINBURGH

CONTENTS

PLATES

INTRODUCTION

THIS book represents a summary of my experience as a runner over the past 13 years. I hope that by publishing it I can put back some of the benefits that the sport has given me and encourage others to take up where I left off.

We are still in a very early stage in putting training on a scientific basis, but I hope that my efforts in this direction will at least serve as a starting point for deeper research. Here I would like to thank Dr Griffiths Pugh for his kindness in reading the chapters concerned with physiology; if there are any errors they are due to my simplifications of very complex matters.

Finally I would like to thank Martin Hyman for his friendship and inspiration ever since the days when we were club runners, my family and friends who have fed me and encouraged me all those years, and most of all my wife Sue, whose love and support has made it all worthwhile.

B. T.

I

Motivation

THE first question that runners are always asked is 'Why do you go in for running long distances at all?' This is a big question, and deserves a reasoned answer. Everyone should be able to justify their actions to other people as well as to themselves, and before spending ten chapters on telling people how to run I feel that I should justify myself for having spent fifteen years of my spare time on it. At the same time I hope I might convey to outsiders the enjoyment of distance running, and encourage those who are just starting to get the best out of it.

To start with, I have always loved to run. Man is built to run; he was a hunting animal for tens of thousands of years before he settled down, first to agriculture then to more sedentary occupations. The joys of walking or running through open country need no advertisement; this is a different matter, however, from the joys of competing in races. This is something which satisfies man's built-in competitive instinct. Over millions of years man has survived and become the dominant species because of his aggressive nature. This can't be turned off like a tap because it doesn't fit in with modern society. When I was at school I was too small for football and had no eye for cricket or tennis. Running was the only physical activity I was any good at, so I did as much running as I could. I got into the school cross-country team, but I was not brilliant. On the track I never broke 5 minutes for a mile or one minute for the quarter-mile. Even so, I got a lot of satisfaction from cross-country by beating boys who were bigger than me.

When I went into the army for my national service I found myself stationed in Hong Kong. There was little to do in the way of work, and sport played an important part in our lives. It was too hot for cross-country most of the year, but there was plenty of track running. Here I found some more of the pleasures of the sport. In the first place, I was a valued member of the team. Our Artillery battery was small in numbers, so anyone with enthusiasm and a bit of talent was welcomed. If I ran well, people noticed. The standard was low, and I got my first taste of the highly addictive drug, success.

This is probably the second-greatest driving force in athletics. What makes the sport so attractive is that success can be achieved without necessarily trampling over anyone else. Because running is a measurable activity, you can see your own improvement month by month and year by year. Success may mean beating your last year's time in a road relay race; it may mean achieving an A.A.A. Grade I standard in your event; or finishing within two minutes of the winner of the national cross-country championships. Whatever your own ability, you can set your own standards of success and work towards them.

Of course there is the struggle between individuals as well, and in this running resembles many other sports—getting in the school or county team, winning a championship, helping your team to win a cross-country race—all these are goals which give meaning to your running.

Success for me meant, first of all, winning the Hong Kong 5000 metres championship, and the thrill of breaking 16 minutes for 3 miles! The first time in a long-distance race, when instead of hanging on grimly, then fading away, I found myself up with the leaders with some reserves still left, was a great experience. The thrill of letting go your final effort, passing your opponents, forgetting your tiredness and hammering up the home straight through the tape is one that the athlete never forgets.

When I went to university at Southampton, I entered another world, with more delights, those of the 'track nut', the dedicated athletics follower. We were only a small group, about a dozen, but the more closely knit because of this. We talked athletics most of our spare time, reading our training diaries, analysing each race, comparing courses and people. It is this enthusiasm which helps one to train hard, and which provides constant incentive to young runners coming into the group. We tried everything; in three years I ran two hundred races, sometimes three in an evening at small club meetings, ranging from 4×110-yds. relays to the Ben Nevis race. Sometimes they were very easy, cross-country against service team races where our team could run in four or five together and then enjoy huge NAAFI teas. Sometimes they were very tough, like the big 9 mile cross-country championship races, where we had to travel for miles, run to exhaustion, fight for a dribble of water to wash off the caked mud, and then embark on the long journey home, sustained by cheese rolls and bars of chocolate because our student grants were running low. The spirit of friendship and shared experiences is one of the things you look back on most warmly in later years.

Of all the races, the most satisfying team race was the Hyde Park Relay. In the normal team race on road or cross-country, the result only appears after the race, by adding up the finishing positions of the scoring men, but in a road relay it is plain to see which team is leading and for this reason road relay races arouse most enthusiasm among distance runners. For the colleges and universities of Britain, the Imperial College race, run in Hyde Park, is one of the peaks of the season. The distance of the lap, a flat 3 miles, means that a half-miler and miler will not necessarily be outclassed by the long-distance runners, while the fact that there are only six in a team means that the small colleges can do well even against the big universities. The planning, the training and above all the selection of who runs what stage are the subjects of much study, while the final results are pored over like the Dead Sea scrolls. In 1957 Southampton had a fine team; I took over on the fourth stage with a string of runners off just before me and came through into the lead which we held to the finish. The satisfaction of that team effort was tremendous.

Distance runners, in temperate countries at least, are very lucky in having a great variety of races in different conditions. In Britain there is hardly a break between the cross-country and the track season; road relays occur in the spring and autumn and road races of every distance from a mile to a marathon go on twelve months in the year. After leaving university most of my running was done as a member of Portsmouth Athletic Club. Here, as at Southampton, we had a good group, whose attitude bred its own success. The planning and the team's programme was worked out by our hard-headed Scots secretary, Andy Gibb; the inspiration came from Martin Hyman, formerly my colleague in the Southampton University team. Martin is a man who believes in leading by example and he set the pattern by getting into the English team for the 1958 Empire Games, coming fourth in the 6 miles. He would be the first to admit that he has little natural running ability; in addition he has been perennially handicapped by asthma in the winter and hay fever in the summer. For him to reach international level was a triumph of determination and intelligent planning. Following his example I made the British team the year after, and other members of the club followed suit. Eventually we had six British track internationals and five out of our top six cross-country men were England internationals. As a team it has resulted in our winning seven Southern, three English nationals, and three European club cross-country titles in eight years.

This brings me to the greatest motive of athletics, the challenge. To achieve the impossible, to pull yourself up out of nowhere and beat the best men in the world by your own efforts is a goal which is worth trying for, and even if you never quite made it, the trying itself makes it worthwhile. Every step you climb is a small victory, over yourself and over circumstances. In a modern industrial society it is hard to show your own individuality. Through running you can get yourself out of the crowd and achieve something by standards which are recognized all over the world. You can pit yourself indirectly against great athletes of the past. You put yourself to the test in the man-to-man struggle of competition. You learn to overcome pain and to master yourself. This is the challenge that athletics offers to everyone.

There is one last source of motivation which does not come to many, though it may indirectly inspire many others. This is reaching the national team and running for one's country. Whatever one may think about nationalism in politics there is no doubt that in sport it produces some of the greatest feats, and in its small way does help to bring countries together. Before a race one may feel intense rivalry for one's opponents, exaggerated by nervousness, but after the competition there is the feeling of comradeship, of experiences shared, which is usually increased by the wine flowing at the banquets.

Although British teams have no team organization, no national training plan, and very rarely the same captain from one match to the next, there is nevertheless some continuity, some mystique which binds them together, and can help quite an ordinary athlete to rise to an unprecedented level. Since the team members seldom see each other between the last match of one season and the first match of the next, it is often some time before this spirit asserts itself. Unlike a football team, athletes are selected strictly on their individual ability, and it may happen that the most reliable of performers runs badly in the championships and is not picked. Nevertheless, out of the sixty or so that make up a national team, there is a sufficiently large core of athletes who stay in the team for several years. The oral traditions build up and are passed on to the youngsters. When the British team assembles for the first match of the season, some are strangers, some are rivals. Friendships start in small groups, based on people, events or clubs but other connections cut across this; there are little regional groups of Scots or Welsh who stick together, and of university and college friends, particularly from Loughborough, which has made such a contribution to the team in recent years. In a home match the blending may not get very far, but on a tour the spirit builds up, and the tougher the competition the better it gets.

The best example of this in recent years was the way things built up from the Rome Olympics to the Tokyo Olympics. Rome was a veritable Dunkirk for British athletics; for those of us that survived it, nothing could ever be tougher. The year 1961 was a lean one in terms of victories, but gave us a lot of experience. This paid off in 1962 when the successes of the European Championships welded together a fine team. The following year we went on to beat the Russians on Russian soil, the first time this had ever been done. The spirit of Belgrade and Volgograd, which showed that our athletes they were as good as any in the world, helped to inspire their great efforts in Tokyo.

People often say to me: 'What do you think was your greatest race?' There is no single answer to this, because different races give you different things. The ones that give you the biggest thrill are the breakthroughs into new territory. My greatest breakthrough was winning the A.A.A. 3 miles championship in 1959, improving my personal best from 13:46 to 13:31. My most satisfying team win was Portsmouth's first success in the national cross-country, after being runners-up for three years. Probably my greatest physical feat was in setting a United Kingdon and European 6 mile record of 27:23·8 in 1966, a time equivalent to the 1964 Olympic 10,000 metres record. Certainly the race which brought me the most fame was the 1962 European 5000 metres championship, and this was also one of my most satisfying races from the tactical point of view. I say one of the most, because at that time I was physically in very good condition, and there is even more mental satisfaction to be gained from winning races by tactical ability when one is not the best in the field physically.

But the race that sticks in my mind as epitomizing the best in running, was in Hamilton, New Zealand, in 1962. I was lucky enough to be invited on the Agfa tour, which at that time was an annual event, along with four American athletes and three Australians. We were to run in a series of six meetings in three weeks, each in a different town or city. The first race was a 5000 metres at Auckland won by Murray Halberg with Barry Magee second and myself third. It was very hot and the times were slow. I was treating the first race as a warm-up, and was pleased with my run, especially in beating Power and Thomas in the last lap. There was a lot of press publicity following the tour, and I happened to mention that I thought I could outsprint Halberg in a finish. This was played up, and the next meeting was featured as a duel between us.

Hamilton is a pleasant town in the North Island, the centre of the dairy area of the Waikato. The hospitality we received there, as we did throughout New Zealand, made us feel relaxed and at home. The track was a grass one, hard underneath and well prepared on top. The meeting was held in the evening; we idled away the morning and dozed in the afternoon. The wind died and the heat went out of the day. From miles around people streamed into the little ground till it was packed to bursting. Perhaps ten thousand people were there, not a large crowd in a big stadium, but in this small arena it created an electric atmosphere. They were treated first of all to a New Zealand 880 yards record of 1:47·1 by Peter Snell, which set a high standard for us to follow.

The line-up for the 2 miles was: Murray Halberg (N.Z.), Olympic 5000 metres champion, and world record holder for 2 and 3 miles; Albie Thomas (Australia), former world record holder for 2 and 3 miles; myself, U.K. and European record holder for 3 miles; Neville Scott (N.Z.), bronze medallist in the Commonwealth Games 3 miles, who was making a come-back; Dave Power (Australia), bronze medallist in the Olympic 10,000 metres and fifth-placer in the 5000 metres; and Barry Magee (N.Z.), Olympic bronze medallist in the marathon, who had finished second in the Auckland race.

From the gun Scott went off at a great pace, 61 or 62 for the first lap and 2:06 for the half-mile. I led the rest through in about 2:08 feeling very smooth and relaxed, closed up on Scott, and reached the mile in 4:17·0. Here it started to become tactical; I thought I could win on the sprint, so didn't want to do all the work; I eased up and let Dave Power come past. He kept the pace going but, with two laps to go, the pace dropped and we closed up into a bunch with Albie Thomas in front. At the bell the time was slow, 7:38·0 for the leader; Halberg came out from behind me and moved up, alongside Power and on Thomas's shoulder. I in turn closed right up on Halberg so that we went into the bend in tight formation. In spite of the roar of the crowd it seemed for a short while calm. I was intensely aware of the mental concentration of the other four men around me, each one waiting for the break. Thomas and Power appeared to have not much left; Scott was barely hanging on; Halberg was the only one who mattered. On the crown of the bend he suddenly accelerated, gaining a couple of yards before I could respond.

In a few strides we were clear of the field and as we went down the back straight I closed up on him. The roar of the crowd in the small space became like thunder, so that Murray couldn't hear whether anyone was behind him. We were both sprinting flat out; as we went into the bottom bend he glanced back, and seeing me on his shoulder tried to accelerate again. I was just able to hang on, but couldn't risk going wide around the bend. Coming into the straight I kicked as hard as I could, but so did he. Up the finishing straight we pounded, our hands clawing the air as if to drag ourselves forwards, and rocking from side to side. I was drawing level, but at an agonizingly slow rate. We covered the last thirty yards with about six inches separating us; we lunged over the line almost together, but I knew Murray had got it. The final times were 8:33·7 for him, a New Zealand record, and 8:33·8 for me, a U.K. record, with Albie Thomas the next man home in 8:37·6. Our last lap was 55·0.

This I feel to be my greatest race not because of the times, which could have been better, but because I felt I had put the best of myself into it, and because I had come so close to beating the Olympic champion in a level race. I have always had a great liking and respect for Murray's iron will, his refusal to be beaten. The exhilaration of that last-lap battle is something I shall always remember.

2

Standards

I HOPE I have made it plain that the better athlete you become, the more you get out of the sport. But although only a few can reach the topmost competitive level, everyone can achieve a high level of fitness if he or she has the will to do so.

We can assume that most people taking up running are not satisfied with their fitness. The first question everyone asks is: 'How can I get fit?' Among many games players there is a belief that fitness is some kind of higher phase of existence, like a state of grace, into which one can be promoted after performing the necessary rituals. What will, I hope, emerge from my chapters on training is that the abilities of the human body, like those of the mind, are capable of almost limitless expansion. Here we shall deal with the extension of only a few of those abilities. One thing is certain, that the 'normal man', by which I mean the average inhabitant of an urban society with a sedentary occupation, is far below the state of fitness of which his body is capable. Of course, fitness means different things in different societies.

In many African states today, as in Britain a hundred years ago, people are quite prepared to walk five or ten miles to market, and children walk up to five miles to school. A million years ago man's survival depended on his running ability.

Today's society makes the least demands on physical performance of any in history. This is not to say that it is unhealthy. People who decry 'physical decadence' ignore the fact that in today's urban societies the expectation of life is longer than in any previous era. However, existence is not the same as living. People who are fit enough to walk to a bus or dig the garden are certainly not fit enough to climb a mountain or run 10 miles; this does not affect their expectation of life but I feel that it does limit their enjoyment of it. This feeling is borne out by medical opinion, which holds that many minor troubles could be avoided if the individual had a higher level of fitness.

Fitness, even in our society, means different things in different sports. To some it means strength, to others endurance, to others speed and co-ordination; most games require different combinations of these qualities.

Until the last few years very few sportsmen made an effort to reach what I would consider to be a high level of fitness. A boxer who has to go for 15 rounds, or a footballer who has to play for 90 min., should be as fit in terms of endurance as any long-distance runner, and if he is a professional he has no excuse. One would not expect him to run a fast 6 miles because it is unlikely that he would have the build for it, but he should be able to run continuously for over an hour. Nowadays the best professional sportsmen maintain high standards of fitness. Amateur sports still vary a lot, but the best rowing crews, especially in Germany and Eastern European countries, do 'out-of-the-boat' training, chiefly running and weight training, which is as tough as that of any distance runner.

Few sports use all the muscle groups all the time, therefore people may be fit in some respects and unfit in others. Here we are concerned with running training, though this does not mean that the aspiring runner should neglect his all-round bodily fitness.

I cannot over-emphasize the possibilities of improvement which the human body possesses. Take a few simple examples. The ordinary man would take 12 or 13 sec. to run 100 yds.; the best sprinter can do it in 9·1. The average man might be able to press overhead about two-thirds of his own body weight—100 lb. for a man 10st. 10 lb. —but the good middleweight lifter can press over 250 lb. A normal man would find it hard to swim half a mile, but a Channel swimmer may swim for between 12 and 20 hours in covering 20–30 miles. Our average man could cycle 15 miles in an hour, but would be tired out and stiff after it, whereas Tour de France cyclists ride over 100 miles a day for three weeks at average speeds of 25–30 m.p.h. You can see from these examples that the difference between the average and the best is fairly slight in terms of speed, much greater for strength and far greater still for stamina. This is because strength and endurance are more easily extended by training.

In distance running, endurance is the most important factor and therefore everyone whatever his basic ability can make marked improvement by training. The question is: 'What standards should we set ourselves?' Our answer to this question is that you should just aim to improve, for once you set a standard you subsequently set limits to your improvement. In the short term, however, it is very satisfying to have targets to aim for and achieve, or a yardstick by which to judge yourself.

Is there an ideal build for a distance runner? Since running involves carrying your own weight over the distance, everyone is in with an equal chance, unless they are overweight. Most distance runners are on the slim side, though men like Kuts, Snell, and Mecser appear to find a well-muscled torso no disadvantage. In the 880 and mile the higher speeds give an advantage to those with a longer stride and specialists at those distances tend to be tall and long-legged, but small men like Derek Johnson, Albie Thomas, and Sydney Wooderson have reached world class.

Long-distance men tend to be small, perhaps because they take it up after having failed at other sports, because their cardio-vascular system is proportionately larger, or perhaps because small men have bigger egos! The only way to find out if you can be a good runner is to try it.

What is a normal untrained performance? The British Army sets a standard time of 6 min. for a mile run in their recruits tests. The Canadian Air Force in their physical training schedule set a time of $6\frac{1}{2}$ min. for a mile run, for flying crew aged 20–25 years. Anyone who can run a mile in 6 min. or faster without training has therefore a chance of reaching a reasonable standard in the sport. Approximately equivalent times would be 440 yds. in 65·0, 880 yds. in 2:30·0, and 3 miles in 20:00·0

It is possible to get an idea of your general endurance fitness, or at any rate your powers of recovery, without running at all. This can be done by carrying out a modified version of the Harvard Step Test, and finding what is known as your Physical Fitness Index (P.F.I.). Measurement of the P.F.I. is best done in pairs, one person being the subject and one the observer, then changing round for another test. The P.F.I. is a measure of your ability to recover from a set exercise. The exercise consists of stepping on and off a 22-in. chair 150 times in 5 minutes (once every 2 seconds). For the test to be valid it is important that the subject steps properly on to the chair, standing straight up, and does not jump on and off. It is permitted to change the leg with which you step on to the chair.

After the 5 min. of stepping has elapsed the subject sits on the chair while the observer takes his pulse. Three pulse counts are taken: P_1 from 1 min.–$1\frac{1}{2}$ min. after finishing the exercise, P_2 2–2½ min., P_3 3–3½ min. The P.F.I. can then be calculated from the formula: $\text{P.F.I.} = \dfrac{15{,}000}{P_1 + P_2 + P_3}$.

It works as follows: a normal person is likely to have quite a fast heartbeat a minute after finishing the exercise; if his pulse is 120 then $P_1 = 60$. After 3 min. his pulse will be nearly back to the normal 72, say 80 a min. therefore $P_3 = 40$. P_2 will therefore be intermediate, approximately 50. Hence P_1 (60) $+ P_2$ (50) $+ P_3$ (40) $= 150$ and P.F.I. $= 100$.

For a less fit person the pulse will remain high for a long time after the end of the exercise, and therefore $P_1 + P_2 + P_3$ will be around the 200 mark, and the P.F.I. reading will be 75. A very fit person will recover completely in the minute before the pulse measuring starts and his $P_1 + P_2 + P_3$ total may be under 100, his P.F.I. reading over 150. The highest P.F.I. I know of is Emil Zatopek's 175 but many other runners have been near that mark.

Assuming that you have some ability, what should you aim for? Aspiring runners should try races of all distances to find what suits them best. Those with the least basic speed will gravitate towards the longer distances where success depends mostly on endurance. You must remember that training will enable you to maintain your pace much longer. Thus, any adult who could run 220 yds. in under 30·0 without training should be able to manage 60·0 for a 440 yds. quite quickly, and 2:00·0 for 880 yds. within weeks or months; after that if he has the inclination and will-power, he could go for the mile and, after all, two halves of 2:00 make a 4:00 mile.

To introduce a personal note into this, the first and only time I ran 3 miles without any training, it took me 18:15. In my first season of competition at the age of 19, having done some training, the best times I could manage were: 440 yds. in 60·8, 880 yds. in 2:12, 1 mile in 4:54, 3 miles in 15:46.

This would be regarded as pretty mediocre by today's schoolboy standards; most schools will have boys of 17 or 18 who can run such times without any training. Since then, by steady progressive training I have reached a state of fitness where I can run a mile at a faster speed than I then averaged for 440 yds., 3 miles at an average speed of 2:12 per 880 yds., and 20 miles at 5:00 per mile speed.

Rates of improvement will vary a lot between individuals. Most runners will start their career while they are still growing and developing, and this makes improvement harder to judge. People who grow taller and stronger will obviously be able to run faster, even without any training at all; others will develop because of the exercise they take in games and in playing, without doing any formal running training. Regular training will usually accelerate progress considerably, for example I have seen a 13-year-old boy improve from 5:46 to 4:59 for a mile in a few months. On the other hand, growth itself may make considerable demands on the energy of a growing child, and training which is overdone may, by causing over-tiredness and lowering the resistance to infection, have an effect which is actually harmful. Because of the pattern of growth, improvement will not always continue at the same rate.

A study of the age-improvement graphs set out below in **Figures 1, 2,** and **3** will show how some of today's leading athletes progressed in their early years. For reasons of space I have only been able to include a few stars in each event and I have deliberately included good-class runners of just below world standard, to give a more realistic measure, particularly where information on their early years is available (see pages 16–18).

A lot can be learnt by studying the improvement of other runners. Firstly you can get an idea of how much you might hope to improve year by year. The starting point will depend on the stage of growth at a given age, as well as on natural ability. Improvement up to the age of 18 is in most cases very rapid; this is because the training effect is added to the effects of growth and development during adolescence.

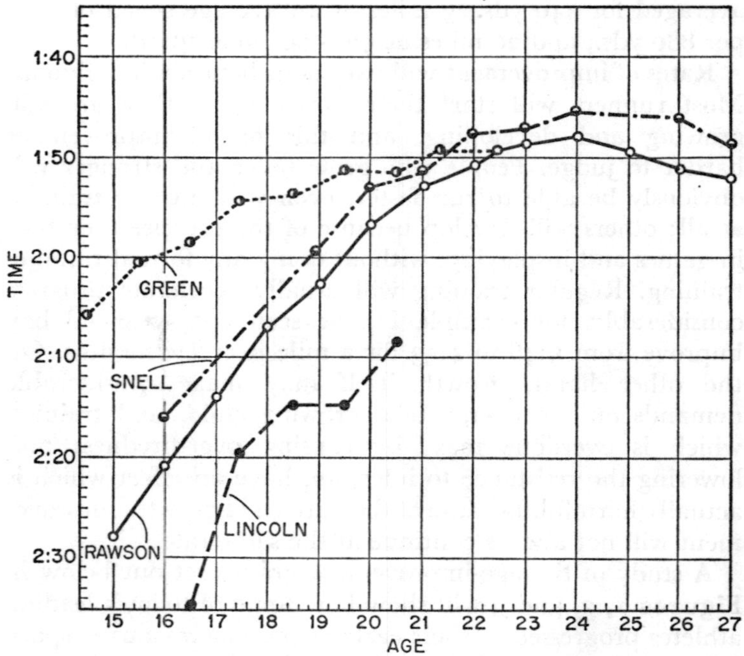

Figure 1   Age Improvement Graph, 880 yds. Andy Green (G.B.), 1967 A.A.A. mile champion; Peter Snell (N.Z.), 1960 Olympic 800 metres champion; Mike Rawson (G.B.), 1958 European 800 metres champion; and Rita Lincoln (G.B.), 1967 W.A.A.A. mile champion.

Looking at the 880 and mile graphs, one can see that between the age of 19 and 21 improvement nearly always slows down and in some cases temporarily ceases. The reasons for this are not hard to find: physical growth ceases at this age, so that the training effect alone remains; the athlete has at this age to face many other problems, such as leaving home and adjusting from school to adult life; at the same

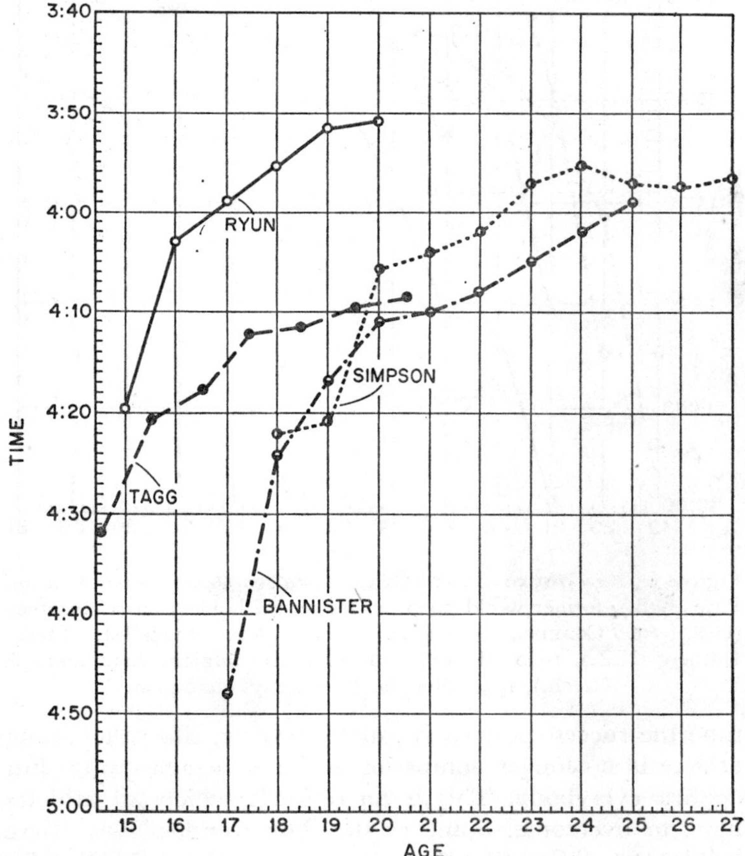

Figure 2 Age Improvement Graph, 1 mile. Jim Ryun (U.S.A.), world record holder; Mike Tagg (G.B.), 1965 A.A.A. junior mile champion; Alan Simpson (G.B.), U.K. record holder; Dr Roger Bannister (G.B.), former world record holder.

17

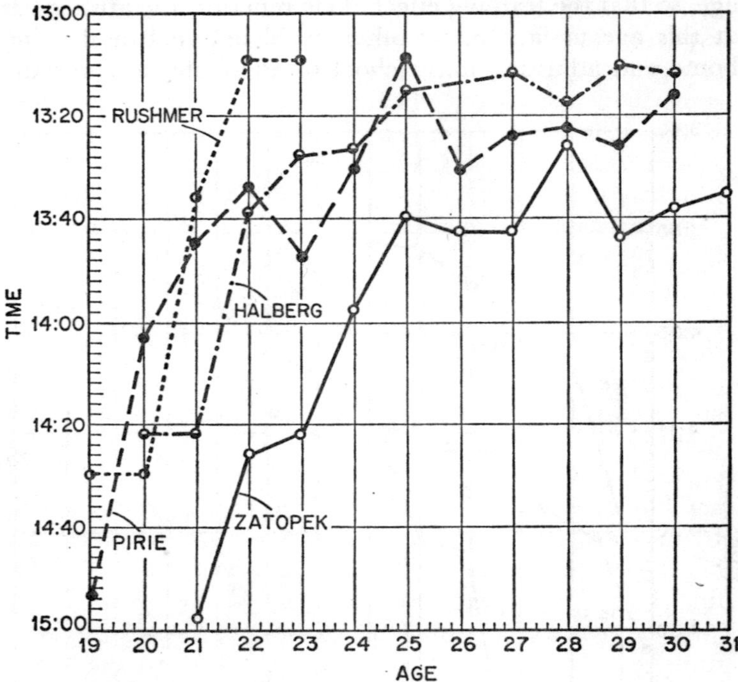

Figure 3   Age Improvement Graph, 3 miles/5000 metres. Gordon Pirie (G.B.), former world 5000 metres record holder; Alan Rushmer (G.B.), 1966 Commonwealth Games 3 miles bronze medallist; Murray Halberg (N.Z.), 1960 Olympic 5000 metres champion; Emil Zatopek (Czech.), 1952 Olympic 5000 metres champion.

time the success pattern is usually broken, since the young athlete is no longer competing in his own age group, but against everybody. This is an obstacle which all athletes have to overcome. Some of the 'boy wonders' who were brilliant at 16 find that they can't go on without the stimulus of constant success. Quite often the 'plodders' who have had to work hard for their progress will persevere and, having got through this difficult period, go on to success in the adult world. Where the rate of improvement is less than might be expected it is an indication to try a longer event. In the 880 graph it is seen that Andy Green's curve has a flatter slope than the others; he has successfully gone on to miling. If one looks at the performances over a mile of top-class long-distance runners it can be seen that the slope of their improvement is flatter than that of the true milers. Looking at the progress shown so far by Mike Tagg, I would say that his future eventually lies in the longer distances, since the angle of his slope resembles that of a distance man.

Lastly you can see that it takes all top-class runners a long time to reach their maximum performance. In making out these graphs I studied the performances of a large number of top-class men. Taking a sample of 10 half-milers I find that the majority of them reach their peak seven or eight years after their first season in the event. Most of this group actually reached their peak between the ages of 23 and 25. In the case of the milers, the majority reached their peak between the ages of 24 and 26, six or seven years after their first season of competition. As might be expected the 3-milers reached their peak somewhat later: out of 12 studied, 10 produced their best mark between the ages of 26 and 30, one at 23, and one at 32. It is interesting to note, however, that on the average this peak was also reached in the seventh year of competition. As the 3 miles is not usually run under the age of 19 this seven years' development brings us up to the 26-and-over peak. I have included in this graph one British athlete who at the time of writing is still in the phase of rapid development. It will be interesting to see whether his graph follows the same pattern as those before him; if it does, he should achieve times below 12:50 for 3 miles, the current world record.

Because of space limitation I have only been able to include the age-improvement graphs of a few athletes; the conclusions I have drawn from them are only a guide, not absolute laws. One finds exceptions like Gerry Lindgren running world class times at 17, or like Fred Norris, setting U.K. records at 38.

Whether or not your own age-improvement graph compares favourably with those athletes shown above, the important thing is to keep on improving. A good way of judging your improvement is against the steps which I have set out below in **Figures 4, 5,** and **6.** In these, the per-

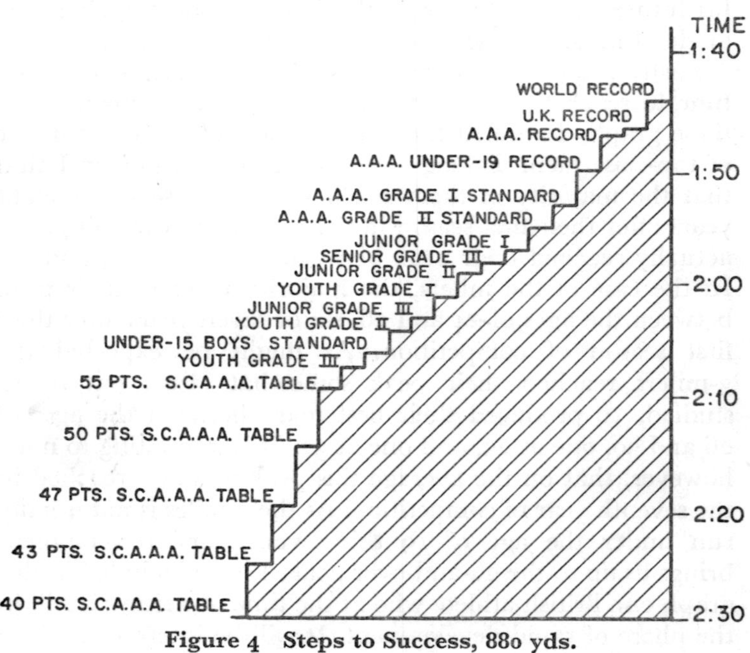

Figure 4   Steps to Success, 880 yds.

formances relate to the end of 1967. The age groups referred to are British ones: Junior means over 17 years and under 19 years on 1 September of the year of competition; Youth means under 17, and Boys under 15. There will be other marks to use as your targets: school, county, or track records.

I have put in as a general guide some of the standards set by the Southern Counties A.A.A. for their Star Award competition for Boys under 16. The top score is 60 points, so that it is

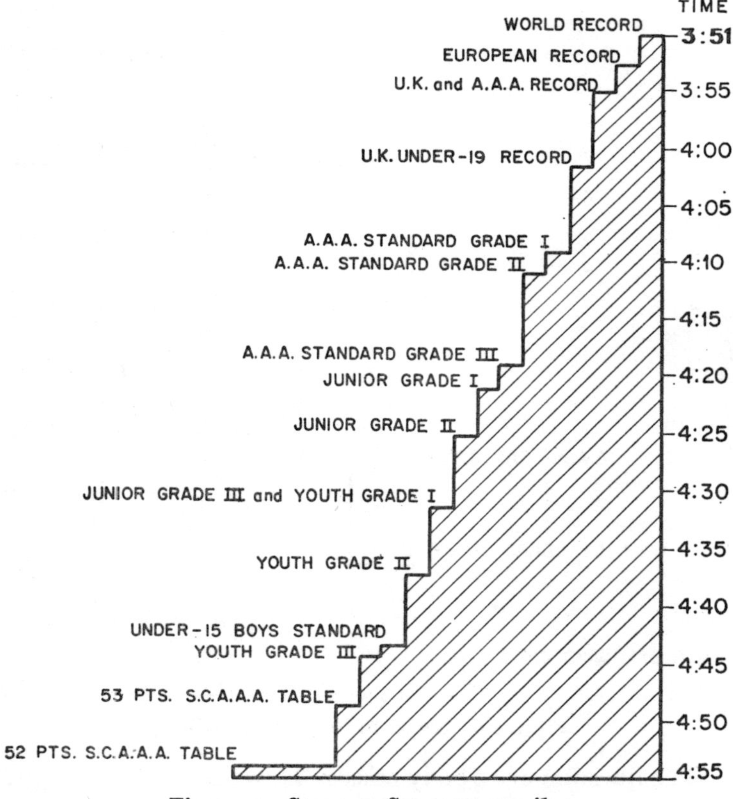

Figure 5   Steps to Success, 1 mile.

possible for most boys to score a few points on the scale; for example a 6-min. miler would score 30 points and a 7-min. miler 11 points. Once you have achieved one step, the next one will seem possible. All the world record breakers had to start somewhere; Jim Ryun's first mile, at the age of 14, was 5:38, and some of today's beginners are tomorrow's record breakers.

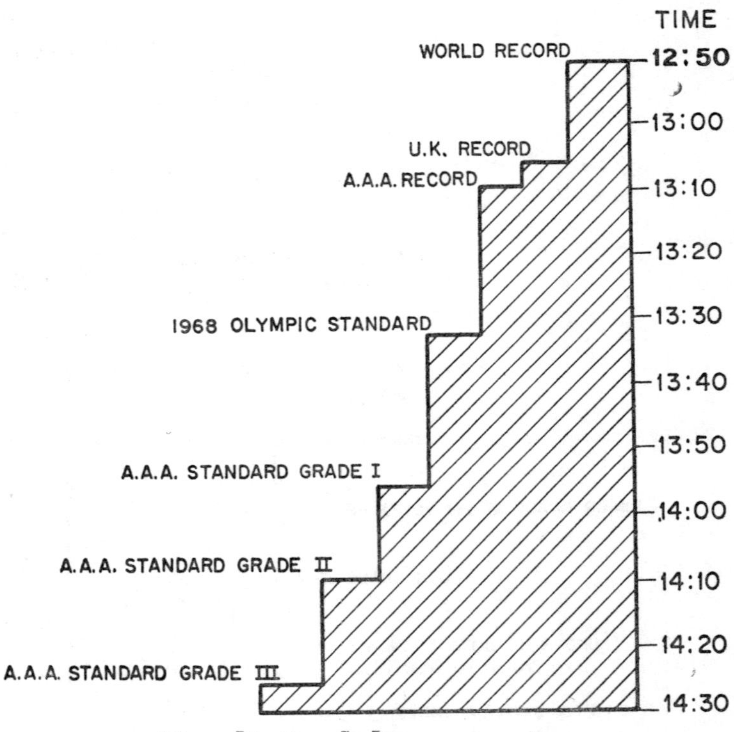

Figure 6   Steps to Success, 3 miles.

The question everybody asks is, 'How far will records go?' Is there an ultimate limit?' Certainly the limit has so far not been reached. It is possible to make predictions, based on past improvements, about the future evolution of records or the raising of standards in a country or in the world. Such predictions made in the past have since been borne out. **Figures 7–11** show the progression of distance records since

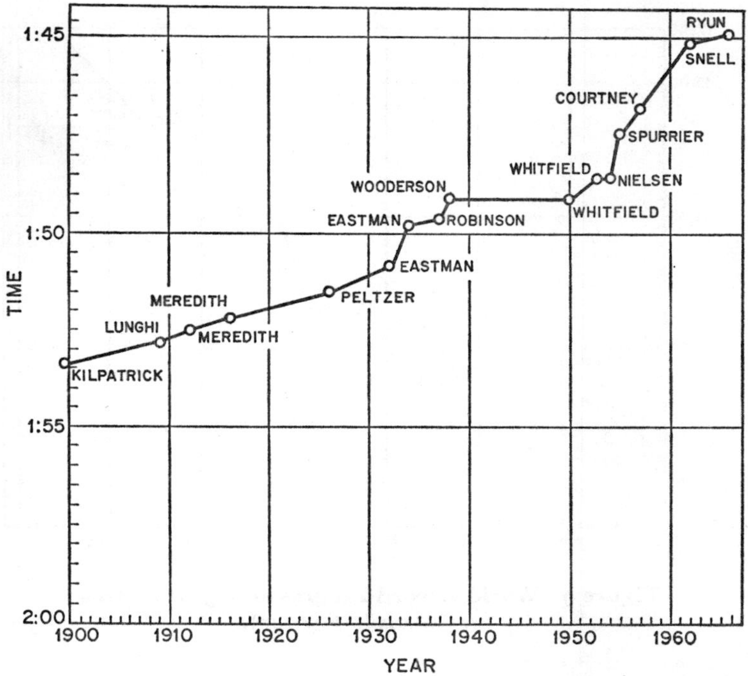

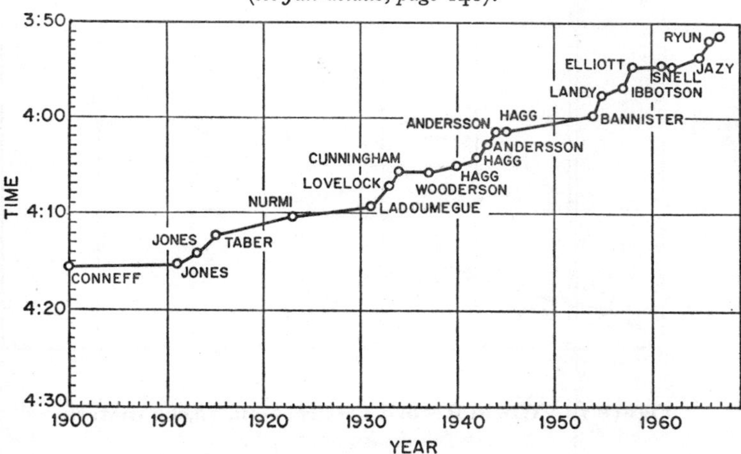

Figure 7   World Record Progression, 880 yds.
(*see full details, page* 146).

Figure 8   World Record Progression, 1 mile
(*see full details, pages* 146–7).

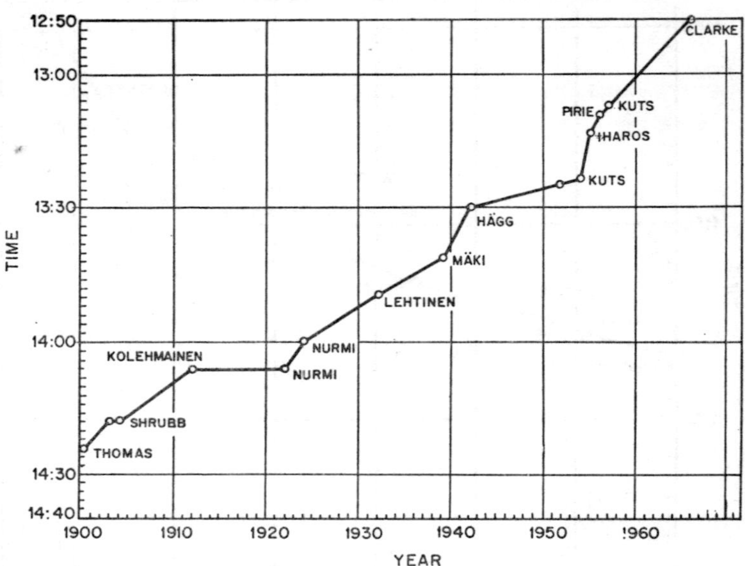

Figure 9   World Record Progression, 5000 metres
(*see full details, page* 147).

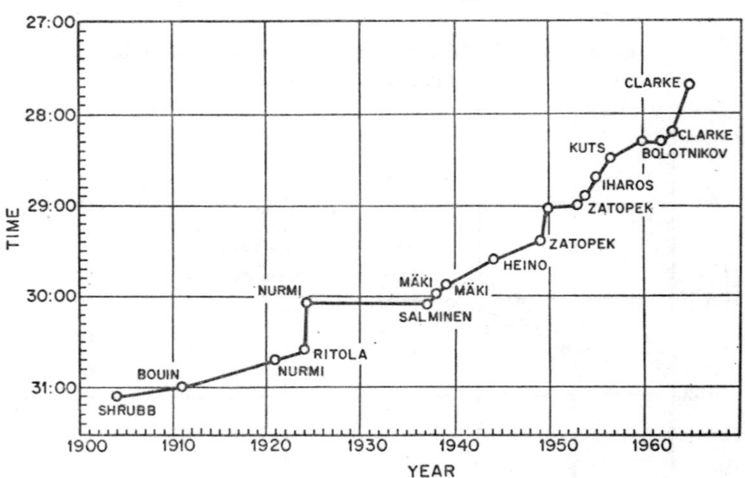

Figure 10   World Record Progression, 10,000 metres
(*see full details, page* 148).

24

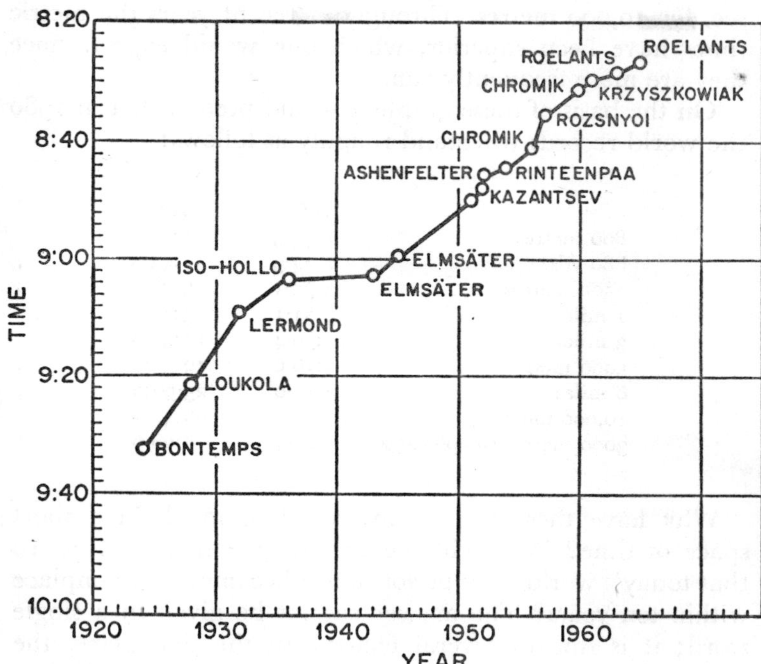

Figure 11   World Record Progression, 3000 metres steeplechase
(*see full details, pages* 148–9).

1900. Full details of world record progression in these events are listed in the Appendix in pages 146–9.

In each of these graphs the probable trends of distance running records from the time of writing to 1980 can be gauged. It can be seen from past development that there are no signs of the rate of improvement flattening out, though this is bound to happen eventually. For the graphs of 3 miles/5000 metres and 6 miles/10,000 metres the superior record has been taken on each occasion, using a conversion of 3 mile time + 28 sec. for 5000 metres and 6 mile time + 60 sec. for 10,000 metres. Throughout recent years the metric times have been superior, which one would expect, since they are more frequently run.

On the basis of these graphs I would predict that in 1980 the world records will stand roughly as follows:

	1967	1980
800 metres	1:44·3	1:42·7
880 yds.	1:44·9	1:43·5
1500 metres	3:33·1	3:28·0
1 mile	3:51·1	3:46·0
3 miles	12:50·4	12:30·0
5000 metres	13:16·6	12:57·0
6 miles	26:47·0	25·50:0
10,000 metres	27:39·0	26:48·0
3000 metres steeplechase	8:26·4	8:08·0

Why have these records improved so much in a short space of time? Why will the records go on improving, so that today's world class performance becomes commonplace within ten years? The answer cannot be given in a single word; it is due to several factors. In the first place, the numbers of people to whom athletics is available has increased a hundred times or more in the past hundred years. In 1870 athletics was indulged in by only a handful of university students in Britain and America. The sport was organized by a small privileged class for their own amusement. If any member of the working classes had the time and the inclination to take part, they would probably have been limited by their low standard of nutrition from reaching a high standard. Of course there were exceptions to this; possibly a strong, well-fed country boy or a lad with natural speed, might by chance discover his ability and break into the world of gentlemen amateurs.

These were the forerunners of a wider participation in athletics. It has gradually spread through the population of

America and Western Europe and Australasia; since 1945 it has been widely adopted in Eastern Europe and is now spreading in South America, Africa, and Asia. Instead of being open to perhaps a million people, it is now the second greatest world sport after soccer. By spreading the net wider, far more natural athletes are found.

The second reason is nutrition. Just as the urban populations of the 19th century suffered from lack of proper diet, so many children in the under-developed countries today do not get enough to eat. In countries where the standard of living has risen, the children are bigger and stronger than their parents, and can make use of the opportunities for sport which are now open to them.

There is also an economic reason, closely linked to the one I have just mentioned. Where people are living a hand-to-mouth existence, time spent on sport is time wasted. When the standard rises a little higher, though, sport is a passport to a better world, a means of getting on in life. The old adage 'hungry men make the best fighters' applies here, though the hunger is for money and security rather than for food. Often a good athlete can get a better chance of a college education. This is certainly one of the reasons for the dominance of Negro athletes in the American team.

All these factors combine to increase the number of athletes trying to reach the top, but do not necessarily produce records. In spite of the increasing competition from Africa and Asia, most of the world records are today still held by Europeans, Australians, and Americans. These people have succeeded because in the face of increasing competition they have trained harder and longer.

Training in the early days consisted of little more than keeping in reasonable health. Great attention was paid to a diet of steaks, raw eggs, and stout. This may have been necessary if the athlete's normal meals were lacking in protein, but would do little for the well-fed middle and upper classes. Exercise was fairly gentle, taking place only in the spring and summer, often including walking and occasionally 'practising' the race distance. It was not long, however, before the competitive spirit began to creep into training. If A and B are disputing the position of top miler in the country and A comes out best, then it is very likely that B will start his training earlier the next year and train a little bit harder, setting his sights on beating A's time.

It is this process which brings the times down. People train harder and more scientifically in order to put themselves on top of the heap. The reason why nobody could run a 4-minute mile before 1954 and now dozens can do it, is that before 1954 it was not necessary to run a 4-minute mile to be the best in the world. Man is a competitive creature but he competes against members of his own species rather than against an arbitrary time standard for an arbitrary distance. Even if someone chooses a time for his target, he is only doing this because it has some relation to what other athletes have done. Man is also a lazy creature; if he thinks he can achieve his object with two hours' training a day, he will not be likely to do four hours' training a day.

Certainly the recent rise in long-distance running standards is directly due to the longer training hours, but there is no reason to think that this will go on indefinitely. After all, the standard events involve running for only 2, 4, 15, or 30 minutes; if training can be made more scientific, there is no reason why in twenty years people should not still be able to lead a normal life and reach world class standards, as they do today.

Inevitably the consideration of rising standards has led us to mention hard training. I hope this does not put anyone off running. I believe that you can enjoy your training and racing at any level. As the work becomes harder the rewards become greater.

Therefore, in the words of the Roman poet[1]: 'Strong of heart, go where the road of ancient honour climbs, earth conquered yields the stars.'

---

[1] Anicius Manlius Severinus Boethius (about 480–524).

3

Making Plans

ONCE you have decided to take up athletics you are immediately faced with the problem of finding the time to train. This is probably the greatest single problem of any aspiring athlete, but it is one which everyone has to come to terms with. You may think that international athletes are not faced with these problems, that they are cushioned and protected by their firms or their college, but this is very seldom the case. The best college athletes in the U.S.A., established internationals in some communist countries, and one or two stars in Western European countries, are lucky enough to have part of their day set aside for training, but all these people had to make their way to the position they have achieved by training very hard in their own time. The majority of athletes in all countries, even those of international standard, have to do a normal day's work or studying as well as their training, and of course they have the same need as other people for normal social and family life. The eventual success of your career will depend quite as much on your ability to balance the various demands on your time as on your actual physical ability.

Athletics is often thought of as needing a lot of dedication, and this is true; some of the schedules I propose later will only be fulfilled by a really dedicated athlete. However, dedication is not the same thing as sacrifice. The idea that to be a successful athlete you must give up everything else is nonsense. In all my years of running the only thing I have consistently had to deny myself is afternoon tea! It takes several years to reach the top class as a distance runner; if you are going to make your life a misery for all that time then the goal is hardly worth the sacrifice. There is no doubt, however, that carrying out a training schedule requires some self-discipline and organization of your daily routine. It will be up to the individual to decide how important running is to him, and how much time he can afford. There is no such thing as not having time to train. Everyone has the same number of hours per day and days per week. How much of that time is spent on training depends on where running comes on your list of priorities.

Basically the young runner must decide which is more important to him at the time—his running or his career. A few brave souls may make the decision that having reached a particular point in their career—for example, having passed school-leaving or university exams—they are prepared to dedicate one or two years wholeheartedly to sport. This is less common in Britain than in Australia, where a year or two devoted to trying to achieve the highest ambition in sport is not regarded as a waste of time. There are dangers in this attitude—it may be difficult to get back into the mainstream of your career after such a break, and you may be a year or two behind your contemporaries—but I would not try to prevent an ambitious young athlete from following such a course. The experience gained will be most useful and the person who is strong enough to take such a step is likely to be able to fend for himself successfully in later life. To such a man I would recommend going to the area where the competition is strongest, finding a job which will give him the best training opportunities while providing enough to live on, and joining the best group of runners in that area.

For the majority, however, it will be a matter of finding a

compromise. Most of us have to make the best of whatever career openings are available in a highly competitive world. Our athletic ambitions may be high, but our talent is modest, so that we are unwilling or unable to gamble our security against the chance of success in a sport which, after all, offers none of the financial rewards of tennis, football, or golf. The athlete is, therefore, left with the basic assumption that his career is more important than his sport; he must now decide how much running he can fit in without affecting his work.

To the school or university athlete this should not be too difficult a problem, since the time-table generally makes provision for sport, but he will have to make a few changes. For a start, running is an all-the-year-round sport; to be successful you need to run at least five times a week. If you can train twice a day on three or four days then you are likely to realize your potential earlier, and will have a bigger platform of fitness on which to build. Secondly, whereas you can play most ball games satisfactorily within an hour or so of finishing a meal, you cannot run really well until two to four hours later. On the other hand there is the advantage that one can train at one's own convenience. An athlete at university or college might therefore follow this type of weekly programme.

Mon. and Wed.	(Games afternoon.) Large breakfast, sandwiches at 11 a.m. Training 2 p.m.–4 p.m.
Tues. and Thur.	Short run before lunch. One-hour session after work, before supper.
Fri.	Rest or easy run.
Sat.	Race.
Sun.	Training at leisure.

The only drawback to this is that there is always study to be done in the evening, when the runner is tired after training. There is no way around this; the alternatives of training first thing in the morning or last thing at night do not suit most people's rhythm of activity; I have found it very difficult to do any useful training at such times. The only thing to do is to transfer the discipline of athletics to your work, give yourself a set task to do and get through it.

The athlete who is no longer studying has a greater problem as it is usually impossible for him to train during the day. If he has a long distance to travel the problem increases. The answers to these problems are not easy, but they do exist. In the first place, he can improve by gradually increasing the quality and intensity of the training which he does after work. Secondly, he can improve his general endurance by putting in an early morning run; many long-distance runners run 5 or 6 miles to work every morning. Thirdly, while maintaining his daily routine at a level which he can absorb, he could boost his fitness by extra-ordinary sessions, either once or twice a week with his club, or with occasional high volume training week-ends. To get the required improvement, however, he must have a definite plan. I cannot emphasize too strongly the necessity of planning. The process of training involves the adjustment of the runner's body and mind to an additional load to which it is regularly subjected; if the intensity and duration of the load are too much, then the body's response will not follow a regular pattern. Let us take for example an athlete of 19. Since leaving school he has settled into a winter routine of going for a run of 4 to 8 miles after work, on the road or in the local park. If he continues to do the same training he will improve slowly over a period of years— perhaps rapidly if he is lucky—depending on a number of other factors such as the amount of competition and his own rate of maturation. To improve more quickly I would recommend him to improve the quality of his training sessions with hill running, *fartlek*, interval and repetition running. If he is temperamentally unsuited to this, and forced to train on his own, I would recommend him to devote one evening a week and one week-end per month or three weeks entirely to running, travelling to a place where he can train with a group and do a really useful session. His other training can then be built around these major efforts, putting his easy days just before and after them.

The following year he could start running twice a day; it would be a mistake to try and increase the quality and the quantity of training at the same time. If training was simply a matter of doing more and harder running than anybody else there would be no need to discuss it. The problem is to find exactly the right balance for each individual, and this balance will vary at different times. Once he has worked out a pattern of living, working, and training the main problem is solved, but there are other minor ones. How often can he afford to miss training? What are the effects of drinking, smoking, late nights? How seriously should he treat colds and coughs? How soon after an illness should he start training again? Although it is impossible to give specific answers, one can lay down general rules. If you plan your training on a weekly or two-weekly basis, then the loss of one training session can be compensated for by increasing the others slightly. Missing one day if you are too busy or too tired is not serious, but if you find yourself missing training frequently then something is wrong with your pattern.

Few modern coaches would condemn the occasional drink or night out. Life is to be enjoyed and running should enrich your life, not restrict it. You will find that the feeling of health which comes from being fit will make you more alive, more capable to withstand stress and also the occasional excess. The effects of a Saturday night out can always be run off on a Sunday morning. The runner must judge for himself, or else his coach must advise him, when and how often he can afford to let himself go and when it is time for abstention and self-discipline. The point is that if he is training hard and regularly he will soon be aware if he is overdoing it in other directions because he will feel more tired than usual in training.

In discussing the plan of life for our athlete, I have assumed that he is getting a good night's sleep and regular meals. A minimum of eight hours a night, preferably nine, is necessary for an adult athlete and longer for a young runner —say ten hours at 16 years old. If you cut down on your hours of sleep, the body will not have time to absorb the training. Instead of improving, you will become more and more tired.

Few athletes in this country should have any worries about diet. We can all afford to eat enough, but whether we eat the right things is less certain. Most of the fallacies about diet stem from the time when the majority of sportsmen were professionals from the working classes, many of whom suffered from chronic malnutrition, particularly lack of protein. In order for them to become fitter and stronger than their opponents, it was only necessary to have a proper diet and take regular exercise. From this came the belief in steaks, milk stout, and raw eggs, which has survived in some quarters to this day. It can easily be shown that what is regarded nowadays as a normal diet, three meals a day, two of them being cooked, seven days a week, contains all the food materials necessary for exercise, growth, development, and repair. Where some people go wrong is in having too monotonous a diet, or in believing that quantity is a substitute for quality. This can lead to a deficiency in vitamin or mineral requirements or sometimes in protein. During hard training the runner will need more protein foods than usual to replace the muscle tissue which is being broken down. These foods—meat, fish, cheese, eggs—will also provide most of the minerals and vitamins needed. Fats and carbohydrates provide the material for producing energy. If the runner is still hungry after his meal, and feels a need for bread, cakes, chocolate, or sweets, then these will help to build up energy reserves for the next day.

It must be borne in mind that the effects of following a sensible way of life only show up over a long period. Eating a lot the day before a race will have no effect whatsoever except that it may upset the digestion and cause loss of sleep. Similarly a restless night's sleep just before a race will not have any adverse effect on your performance unless you worry about it. It is the tensions and inhibitions caused by worrying about such things which have far more effect than the original causes. There are many good athletes around who have never achieved their full potential because they worry too much about minor troubles.

The runner may often come across opponents who appear to have some magic ingredient for success such as glucose before a race, vitamin tablets every day, rabbits' feet under the pillow. The first two have generally as much effect on his performance as the third would have. Since the level of blood sugar is maintained at a constant level by the action of the liver, taking glucose before a race will have no effect on that race (though it may help the athlete to recover more quickly after it). Unless one is suffering from a vitamin deficiency, taking vitamin pills is literally pouring money down the drain, since the unwanted vitamins pass straight through the body.

The basic rules are simple; the athlete needs a plentiful and varied diet, regular hours of sleep, and hard training.

4

Training—Basic Principles

You must run till you feel tired, and then keep on running. All modern training is based on the overload principle according to which the body, if subjected to an increased load, will gradually adjust itself until it is strong enough to cope with the task. If the load is increased steadily the body will steadily become stronger, but if it is increased too quickly the body will be weakened and illness or injury will be the result.

This is the basic situation, but it is complicated by the fact that there are several different factors involved in distance running, none of which can be neglected. In preparing a training programme we must therefore seek to improve all the various factors at the same time, while the total load must not be too much for the body to stand. When the athlete has learned what he can take, he must then raise his training targets so as to increase the load steadily through the training session.

I would like first of all to run through the physiological principles involved, as this is necessary to understand the reason for doing different kinds of training. There is always a lot of mystique surrounding training schedules—some appear to work, but when applied to a different person they have little effect. Many athletes seem to believe that there is some sort of magic formula which if it were whispered in their ear would transform them overnight. Training is at once more mundane and more challenging than that.

Emil Zatopek has said: 'By a persistent effort of will it is possible to change the whole body.' The athlete must always keep in mind this concept of change and progression; he must never accept his limitations as being permanent, because they are not.

What happens when we run? The muscles receive commands from the brain via the central and peripheral nervous systems. They respond to the stimulus by contracting; these muscular contractions work the lever system, which is made up of our bones and joints, to move the body forwards. The initial speed of movement will depend on how many muscle fibres contract in response to the initial impulse, and to a lesser degree on the extent to which the rest of the body impedes the action of the working muscles.

The energy for the muscular contraction comes from the breakdown of phosphate compounds, quantities of which are stored in the muscle fibres. These compounds themselves are re-formed by the energy provided by the breakdown of glucose, which is carried to the muscles in the blood. The glucose concentration is kept up to a fixed level, being renewed from the glycogen store in the liver. As a result of glucose breakdown, lactic acid accumulates in the muscles. All these reactions can take place without the use of atmospheric oxygen, so this phase of energy production is known as 'anaerobic'.

The lactic acid which accumulates would soon bring the process to a halt, were it not converted back into glucose. To provide the energy for this reconversion, one-fifth of the lactic acid is broken down to carbon dioxide and water, using atmospheric oxygen transported by the haemoglobin of the red blood corpuscles. The energy from this breakdown converts the other four-fifths back to glucose. The end products of respiration (carbon dioxide and water) are removed by the bloodstream and expelled by the lungs. During very intensive exercise, however, both lactic acid and carbon dioxide will accumulate in the body causing discomfort, pain, and eventual collapse.

In the conditions of a race, the athlete is performing at far above the normal level. His ability to do this is greatly increased by the action of the hormone, adrenalin, which has several effects. It increases the rate of the heartbeat; it causes the blood supply to the digestive system to shut down, and that to the muscles to increase; it enables the liver to release a supply of glycogen which is normally 'locked up' and unavailable; it also helps the athlete to endure more discomfort than he would normally be capable of.

We can now see some of the physiological factors affecting running performance. The main ones can be listed as follows:

(1) A large muscle, i.e. a large number of muscle fibres.

(2) A good nerve-muscle response, i.e. contraction of the maximum number of fibres in response to a nervous stimulus.

(3) Flexibility in the joints and the antagonistic muscles, to produce the minimum opposition to forward movement.

(4) A high level of the energy-producing phosphates in each muscle fibre.

(5) A high level of blood-sugar.

(6) A large store of glycogen to keep up the level of blood-sugar.

(7) An efficient oxygen absorption system, i.e. well-developed lungs, with rapid diffusion through the lung membranes.

(8) An efficient oxygen transport system. This involves (*a*) a high red-blood corpuscle count and haemo-globin content, (*b*) well-developed blood supply to

the muscles (high capillarization), and (*c*) a large, strong heart.

(9) Ability to tolerate a high level of lactic acid and carbon dioxide in the muscles.

(10) A rapid release and continuous supply of adrenalin.

(11) Efficient 'cell chemistry' to carry out the cycle of reactions with the maximum speed and the minimum quantity of by-products.

(12) A robust nervous system which will function efficiently even in a state of fatigue.

What we have now to consider is how the training we do brings about improvement in these factors. The way in which the body responds is not fully understood, but coaches and athletes have discovered by empirical methods that certain types of training bring about certain effects. The physiological proof of how the changes are effected still lags a long way behind.

Now it might be possible to improve considerably by going out each day and trying to run a mile as fast as possible. At one time this is just what athletes did. The drawback here is that in order to approach the conditions of a race, the athlete would have to work up great excitement and secrete a lot of adrenalin. This would be very difficult to achieve more than once or twice a week, and the nervous strain involved would decrease the amount of training possible. The logical way is to try and improve one or two factors at a time; it is easier to break a bundle of sticks one by one than all at once.

To determine what type of training is needed to develop which factors we must remember the overload principle—that the body will react so as to adjust itself to increased effort. The particular factor which needs developing most will depend on the athlete's event, and his own limitations.

Many of the training activities normally done will affect

several factors simultaneously. In general, the closer the athlete gets to simulating the conditions under which the race is run, the more of the limiting factors will he be extending.

Which of these factors is most important to the runners? As far as we know at present, the factors which decide how good an athlete is going to be are the oxygen transport system and the ability of the body to tolerate lactic acid. To give an example, there is a direct relationship between the speed of running and the amount of oxygen taken in; the maximum amount taken in per minute can be measured for each athlete. In a series of treadmill experiments done in Sweden in 1966, it was found that, at a particular speed, Ron Clarke was working at a much lower percentage of his maximum intake than anybody else. Thus in a long-distance race he would be accumulating his oxygen debt much less quickly and would be able to go on for longer.

Analysis carried out at the end of long-distance races has consistently shown that the leading runners, although presumably fitter than the others, were in a worse physical condition; their body temperature was higher, their blood-sugar content lower, and their lactic acid concentration higher than runners further down the field. This is the physiological proof of the observed fact that, other things being equal, the man with the strongest motivation—the man who can push himself the hardest—will win the race.

This ability to tolerate pain, which is what it amounts to, is, of course, closely linked with the adrenalin supply. There are many examples of athletes who are no better than their fellows when training, even though they may be trying hard, yet show up to great advantage in a race. The only source of their sudden improvement relative to the others is in their reaction to the nervous strain of racing. It is known that the action of the sympathetic nervous system is such that it can simultaneously give impulses which stimulate muscles and impulses which inhibit muscle action. One athlete may suffer from nervous inhibition before a race, while in another the muscle will respond more readily than usual. In both athletes some adrenalin will be produced, but in one it will be far greater. The effect of the adrenalin is to stimulate both his rate of heartbeat and the volume pumped at each stroke, to mobilize more sugar from the liver to the blood and to increase his tolerance of pain.

I have said that these factors are the most important, because there is good evidence that as they are developed so the runner improves. Of the other listed factors, 4, 5, and 6 do not appear to be very susceptible to improvement by training, though a deficiency in respect of one of these might prevent a runner from reaching a high standard.

Lung size (factor 7) does not appear to be a limiting factor. Although the lungs develop during training, this appears to be only a side effect, not an essential. The vital capacity of the lungs differs widely in different individuals, and does not appear to be correlated with running ability, once the training effect is taken into account. However, recent research done on runners at high altitude indicates that the diffusion rate of oxygen into the lung membranes may be a limiting factor, but how it is affected by training is not yet known.

Factors 2 and 3 will be developed during training as side effects of training done for other purposes; they are both aspects of skill training which is of more importance in other athletic events than running. The running action is a simple and natural one, and the ability to perform it correctly does not in my opinion need any special training.

The first factor, that of muscular strength, is of greater importance in throwing and sprinting events, but should not be ignored by the middle-distance runner. Increase in basic speed is dependent on increase in muscle strength, and sheer sprinting speed is often of vital importance in deciding who gets the gold medal and who the silver. Furthermore, as we shall see in the section on tactics, a slight superiority in basic speed may have a far greater psychological effect in determining the runners' attitudes to each other, and hence the tactics employed The most direct way of improving strength is by weight training, using progressive resistance exercises.

The last two factors, 11 and 12, are very much imponderables; much research has still to be done in these areas. It is my own view that the reasons for general endurance are bound up with these factors. In a long-distance race the athlete is for much of the time working at a rate at which he can take in all the oxygen he needs. The oxygen debt, after a quick increase in the early part of the race, remains pretty well constant, rising again sharply when the pace increases at the finish. During the intermediate period the things which will decide his pace is the efficiency with which his muscles are working. As the race continues, there will be accumulation of fatigue products in the muscles; the internal body temperature will increase; the energy reserve in the liver will decrease and may have to be augmented from other sources. The oxygen debt accumulated in the early part of the race may affect all these processes. Under these conditions the brain and the nervous system must continue to send out orders to many parts of the body, and the muscles must obey them. How can the athlete ensure that the system will work with the maximum efficiency?

In the next chapter I propose to examine the various training methods now in use, and see what benefits they give in improving the limiting factors.

5

Analysis of Training Methods

EVERY kind of exercise will be of some benefit to an athlete, but since time is limited he must select those activities most useful to his purpose. From the historical point of view training has progressed considerably, mostly in the direction of increased intensity, but also of increased quantity. Is there a maximum amount of training which can usefully be done? What is the minimum one can get away with? The answer will differ for each individual. For example, I know one cross-country runner, approaching 40, who continues to produce high-class performances at national level on only 35 min. of running a day, regularly beating athletes ten to fifteen years younger who are training 80–100 miles a week. In spite of this, both these types of training are right for the person doing them. The elder man, a great natural athlete, has over many years made his body a 'running machine' of great efficiency. He is now concerned only with keeping himself going at that level and devotes the rest of his time to his family and his business. The younger athletes, doing a large volume of training, are trying to induce the training effects as quickly as possible, doing as much as time will allow and their bodies will stand.

Continuous Running
The simplest and most obvious activity is continuous running. To the unfit person, even running half a mile without

stopping is an effort. For the beginner and for the young athlete, continuous running will bring about a rapid improvement in the heart-lung system which can be measured by a decrease in the pulse rate taken at rest. It will accustom the nerve and muscle system to prolonged work. It will also enable the runner to find the stride-length which suits him best and a natural breathing rhythm, both of which will soon become automatic. As these factors improve he will find himself able to run for a longer time at each outing. If he has a circuit to run round he will find that he can run it in a given time with less effort, or with the same effort in a shorter time.

To the serious athlete, however, merely going for a run is not training. Continuous slow running alone will not bring about continuous improvement, except possibly in the case of marathon runners. The reason for this should now be obvious; it is that slow running does not affect many of the limiting factors in races. However, since it does affect general endurance it still forms part of training for most runners. Even a half-miler needs general endurance, especially when he may be expected to run heats, semi-finals, and finals in quick succession. Any adult runner, in the events we are considering, should be able to run 10 miles continuously without ill effects, at any stage of the season, and a 3- or 6-miler should be able to cope with a 20-mile run. Apart from the benefit to the general endurance, it is thought that by continued use the proportion of capillary blood vessels in the leg muscles increases, and this means that when the muscle is under stress the blood supply and hence the oxygen supply will be greatly increased.

The other use for slow, easy running is during the racing period. At this time the athlete does not need any hard training—it is too late to have any effect on the next race. Since he is accustomed to regular training, however, he may become subject to doubt if he stops completely.

Replacing his normal hard training by easy running will enable him to keep his normal rhythm of eating and sleeping. Before a race it will help him to concentrate on the on-coming struggle. It is a good idea to train for a few days before each race at the same time of day as the race will take place. This will help the runner to become accustomed to the weather conditions likely to be expected and mentally prepare him to make an effort at that time.

Lastly, after a hard race, easy running is useful in restoring a relaxed mental and physical condition. The repetition of a simple enjoyable routine will help to ease both the tired muscle and the tired mind.

For the time being I shall leave the consideration of fast continuous running, which is quite a different matter.

Fartlek

The next step up from slow running is to put in patches at a faster pace, interspersed in the long slow runs. This was the system used by many of the great Scandinavian runners and is known as *fartlek*, meaning 'speed play'. It is infinitely variable, and can really cover a whole range of different kinds of training. What we normally understand by the term is a continuous run in which patches of fast striding are interspersed with jogging. The fast bursts may be of any distance from 50–1000 metres or more; the slow running is generally of equal or greater distance, to allow for complete recovery before the next fast burst. The pace of the fast burst will be a good deal less than flat-out for the distance covered, but should always be well above the pace of a steady run, that is to say, while the athlete is doing the fast burst he should find it getting harder towards the end, rather than just settling into a slightly higher rhythm. In true *fartlek* the recovery running should go on until the athlete feels quite recovered, i.e. his breathing will have returned to its normal rhythm and his oxygen debt will have been paid back.

The benefits of this type of training are many. In the first place it is a very good way of introducing a young or inexperienced runner to good quality training without making it seem too severe. Once some basic fitness has been acquired by jogging it is natural to want to run fast even if only for a short period, and this can easily be exploited. During early-season training runs, done in a group, the leader can say, 'We'll run steadily up to the top of the hill and stride out on the way down'. With the incentive of being in a group, and with only a short distance to run, the athletes will find themselves running quite hard without making a great mental effort. The athlete who had to run alone can fix points along his regular runs between which he will increase his speed.

I have found from experience that after having several 50–100-yd. strides in the first few minutes of the run by way of a warm-up, it is easiest to start off with the long bursts, perhaps 660 or 880 yds., and then reduce the distance, so that at the end of the run one is only doing 100 yds. in each burst, but at quite a fast pace.

If done in a progressive fashion, this training will bring several benefits. The frequent changes in rhythm will accustom the muscles to sudden stimulation (factor 2, page 00). The acceleration at the beginning of each burst will increase the size of the muscle (factor 1), while the whole lever system becomes accustomed to operating at this pace (factor 3). The greatest and most easily measurable benefit will come in the oxygen transport system (factor 8).

The increase in the number of red-blood corpuscles and in the blood supply to the working muscles cannot be measured without special equipment, but there is no doubt that it does occur along with the increase in size and strength of the heart. Since the heart is a muscle, it will obey the same laws as other muscles: the more it is subjected to exercise the stronger it will become. This fact was clearly demonstrated by the work of men such as Prof. Reindell and Woldemar Gerschler with heart patients. They found that running which required the heart to beat faster brought about a much more rapid strengthening of the heart than took place in patients leading a so-called normal life. The benefits of running to the unfit 'normal' person has been shown by the success of Arthur Lydiard's Jogging Club in Auckland, where men of middle age and even old age brought about considerable improvements in their general health by gentle but increasing exercise.

In the case of our distance runners following the *fartlek* system, the increased pace in the fast bursts will require an immediate increase in the rate of heartbeat. As the heart strengthens in response to this need, over a period of weeks, it will become capable of dealing with its normal task much more easily, and when at rest the pulse beat per minute will become lower. From an average for the adult of 72, higher in young people, it will decline with training to below 60, and, in a very fit distance runner, to well below 50.

If the athlete has sufficient will-power to drive himself it is quite possible he could reach world standards by *fartlek* training alone. In fact, there are athletes who have done this, but the system has some drawbacks. In my view the essence of *fartlek* training is that it is a voluntary form of effort: the athlete can ease up when he feels tired. Since he is likely to get lazy in training at times, as we all do, there will be occasions in a *fartlek* run when his bursts are well below maximum and his recovery periods very long, so that he is not making the best use of his time. On the other hand, if training is done in groups, *fartlek* can become competitive with runners racing out each burst. This may be good for the best runners in the group, but it is certain to be harmful to the less able runners, who will find themselves doing harder training than they can absorb. The other drawback is that without great application of will-power the athlete will not go on running for very long in a state of fatigue, when the body is forced to accustom itself to tolerate lactic acid and carbon dioxide.

Interval Training
The logical development from this is interval training, which must still form the centre of any progressive training plan. In interval training the speed and duration of the fast burst, the duration of the recovery period and the total extent of the training can all be planned in advance, measured accurately and recorded afterwards. This means that the athlete can see his own progress and, making allowance for external conditions, can compare his present performance with that in previous years and with the performance of other athletes.

Interval training can, and should, be done on an individual plan, since it can be tailored exactly to the individual's needs. Since it is usually done on a track, however, it is often possible to share a session with other athletes and thus make the mental strain much lighter.

The distances run in interval training will normally be from 100–880 yds. The recovery period will depend on the fitness of the athlete. It has been found that to produce the most rapid strengthening of the heart the exercise should be sufficiently severe to push the pulse rate up to about 180. Since at the end of races the pulse goes up to over 200, the intensity of the fast run in interval training is just below an all-out effort. The length of the recovery time should be sufficient for the pulse rate to drop to the beginning of the 'plateau level', which is about 120 for most athletes. It is important for each athlete to find out how long he takes to recover since, if he is taking too short a recovery rate, he is going to lose the benefits and get over-tired. This will apply particularly in the case of a young runner training with people who have reached a higher level of fitness. He may need, say, 2½ min. to recover from the previous fast 440 while they are starting again after only 1½ min. If he tries to complete the session he will not get as much benefit as he would from a session geared to his own recovery rate since, during most of the recovery period, his pulse will still be in the 160–180 range, and during the fast run it will go up to over 200. At this very high rate the volume pumped at each stroke tends to diminish, and the strengthening effect on the heart is decreased. It must always be remembered that it is in the recovery period that the effects of training accrue; the heart is a muscle, and having been stretched it will, during its rest period, gradually strengthen itself to meet the strain. To do this, extra food materials have to be brought in the blood vessels supplying the heart walls. If they are passing through too quickly, then there will not be time for them to be used.

Sticking purely to the heart-training effect of interval running, it would appear that the more times the pulse rate is stimulated and allowed to recover in each training session the better, i.e. the fast portion should be very short, 100 or 220 yds. only. This may be true for heart patients, but for athletes, as we know, other factors have to be developed along with the heart, and these can only be developed if the pressure is kept up for some time. On this theory, to take an extreme example, the best way to train for a 4:00 mile would be to run for as long as possible at a speed of 60·0 per 440 yds., and then repeat the effort as soon as possible. The physical limit requires an immense mental effort, and it would not be possible to do this type of training every day. By training over distances of 330, 440 or 660 yds., the conditions of pressure are simulated for a short time towards the end of each fast run. The distance run is short enough for the effort to be repeated frequently without great mental strain.

If the recovery interval is fixed by the pulse rate, we have to decide on the distance of the fast run, its speed, and the number of repetitions. Most runners find it hard to do a large number of repetitions when the distance is over half a mile, and if it is less than 220 yds. then there is not enough time for the pressure to build up. We therefore work over distances between these two extremes. I myself use a great variety of different distances, so that I never have to repeat a session more than once in two weeks.

To fix the total volume and the speed of a session one must decide on what one is training for. As a rough guide one could say that the total distance covered in fast running should be more than the racing distance, but not more than twice as much. The 'heart-training' effect will be induced in all types of interval training, though to a differing extent; if one trains over short distances run at a fast speed, the main benefit will be in the 'muscle metabolism'—the ability of the muscle to work efficiently at speed. If the bursts are done over longer distances at a slower speed, then a smaller proportion of the session is taken up with recovery periods, and more work is done in the session; the main benefit is therefore a gain in general endurance. If you set the total amount of work at about the distance of the race, and the speed at that of your best race, and then take the shortest possible recovery period, then you will be doing 'special endurance' training. A proper training programme will naturally include interval work of all three types.

The main drawback of interval running is its monotony. It must therefore be varied as much as possible, so that the runner comes fresh to each session, regarding it as a challenge and not as drudgery. Once or twice a week on the track, to measure progress, is quite enough. The other sessions can be done on grass, roads, sand, or over cross-country circuits.

An experienced athlete will soon learn to judge the speed at which he is running and the recovery he needs, so that only the distance and number of repetitions need be recorded. Personally, I like to use a watch in most of my interval sessions since, even if I do not know the exact distance I am running, round a cricket field for example, I can still measure improvement month by month and year by year.

I hope that from what I have written it can be seen that there is no direct answer as to whether one type of interval session is better than another, since all will have different effects. For example, one can combine a stamina session with some fast 220s at the end and then get an added speed benefit. The 'Hungarian' type of training, used by Igloi when coaching his group of world record breakers in the fifties, involved training at fast speeds with short intervals, but with only a few repetitions in each group. By doing two or three sets of intervals of this type in each session punctuated by a rest of several minutes, and by doing two sessions a day, he was able to combine a general endurance effort with the muscle metabolism and special endurance effects already gained. The drawback to this type of training is that it needs a large portion of the day to carry it out.

As a general point, it is better to decide on a particular type of interval training at the beginning of the year and then try to improve on it in one direction only, rather than try to do several things at once. For example, a 3-miler aiming at 13:00 (65·0 per 440 yds.) could start off in several ways: (*a*) running 65·0 per 440 with a minimum interval of, say, 45·0, and increasing the number done in each session; or (*b*) doing a set number, say twenty, 440s with a fixed interval, starting at a relatively slow speed, say 68·0 per 440, and trying to improve his average to below 65·0; or (*c*) doing a set number at a set speed, say 20 × 440 in 65·0, but with a long interval between them, and then trying to cut down the interval.

Any one of these methods can show an improvement as the year progresses. On a year-to-year basis one can, and should, make the sessions progressively harder by improving other aspects, i.e. aiming at a shorter interval, greater volume, or greater speed than in the previous year.

Many runners feel that they cannot do interval training unless they have a track to run on. This is nonsense. It is the effort which counts, whatever the conditions underfoot. For the town-dweller, quiet roads under street lights make an excellent winter training ground, while those lucky enough to live in the country can run on fields or paths as well. When the evenings are light enough, most people can find a patch of grass or playing field, and work out their intervals on that. Absolutely accurate distances are not necessary, nor is exact measurement of each session. You can work out the distance in terms of time, e.g. one minute fast, one minute jog, or in terms of paces, e.g. 200 paces fast, 200 paces jog, or between fixed points on a circuit.

Interval training has a great advantage in getting a lot of useful work in a short time, and therefore is bound to form the staple diet of athletes who have to work or study as well, which means 99 per cent of the athletes reading this book.

When Rudolf Harbig broke the world 800 metres record with 1:46·6 in 1939, one of the greatest athletic feats, measured against his own generation, which has ever been performed, it might have been thought true to say that in the interval training he did, scientific training had reached the ultimate. Since then, not only have athletes broken Harbig's record, using other systems, but in the longer events records have been completely revised. In the 5000/10,000 metres range Emiz Zatopek, using interval training, led the breakthrough. Kuts and Bolotnikov, using faster speeds and shorter intervals, lowered the records further. At the time of writing these records have succumbed to a whole group of runners—notably the great Ron Clarke, Keino,

Norpath, and Jazy—working under different systems in different places. The moral of this is not only that the ambitious spirit will continue to drive the body to greater limits, but also that even the immensely versatile interval system is not enough on its own.

I now want to examine some of the other types of training.

Repetition Running

This is a form of training which merges with interval training at one end, and at the other reaches its climax in time-trial running. The difference between repetition and interval training is that there are long periods of rest between the fast runs. These periods are long enough to allow so-called 'complete recovery' which means far more than just restoration of the pulse to the 'plateau' level. In the long recovery period the lactic acid is completely dissipated and the blood-sugar returns to its original level. The fast runs are generally over longer distances than in interval training, and, if at the same distance, then they are done much faster, e.g. a miler might be running his interval 440 yds. in 62·0 each, with $1\frac{1}{2}$ min. rest, and his repetition 440s in 56·0, with 5 min. rest. A 6-miler might do repetition miles in 4:40 instead of interval 440s in 70·0.

The benefits of this type of training are, for the shorter distances, benefits in the muscle metabolism (efficiency of the muscle at racing speeds), and for the longer-distance runner, in the tolerance of lactic acid and other poisons. This is special endurance work, simulating race conditions, and reaches its climax when one does time-trials: a simple effort, flat-out, over perhaps half to three-quarters of the racing distance.

There is no doubt that this type of training brings success; many athletes become adept at interval training, but never become sufficiently accustomed to the discomfort experienced in the middle of a race to be able to overcome it successfully. It does, however, require a lot of will-power. For this reason I do not recommend its use to young athletes and only infrequently to older ones. Too much suffering in training is, I feel, a denial of the word 'sport', and if it kills the enjoyment of racing then it may do more harm than good to the performance.

However, people have devised ways of getting through a lot of work by making hard training enjoyable. A lot is talked about the mental factor in running, and this is its second most important aspect. If, by having the right coach, the right surroundings, and the right people to train with, runners can look forward with enthusiasm to their training, then the battle is half won already. Even if we cannot all live in 'ideal' surroundings, there is usually something which can be done to introduce variety.

The successes of first Herb Elliott and then Peter Snell brought home dramatically to European coaches the need to get away from the track, to become tougher and less inhibited. But these men were really only the most successful exponents of a trend which has always been prevalent among British distance runners. The success of one man can be attributed to many things, but the mark of a successful system is the production of a constant stream of top-class men. The tremendous depth of British runners in the 5000/10,000 metres range is largely due to the British weather, which enables cross-country running to flourish throughout the winter months. It can be argued that the intensity of winter competition may prevent individuals from attaining such a high level of performance in the summer, but there is no question that the system does produce a lot of good athletes.

Hill, Cross-country, and Resistance Training
Drawing on this tradition, what are the extra factors which are needed in a complete training system, to add to a basis

of *fartlek* running and interval training? There are several to be considered: hill training, cross-country running, and what I call 'resistance work'; that is to say, running through sand, snow, or plough, or running in boots.

Running uphill has an easily defined effect; it strengthens the stomach, thigh, and ankle muscles, producing the same effects as sprint training, but more rapidly. My own view, based purely on intuition, is that hill running should be done at a fairly fast speed, so that as the new muscle fibres are built up, they are accustomed to rapid expansion and contraction.

Cross-country running, as opposed to racing, will provide a greater all-round strengthening effect than pure road or track running. The effect appears in the strengthening of those muscles and ligaments which assist the maintenance of posture. These are often forgotten in the consideration of running movement, but a considerable amount of energy is expended in keeping the body balanced while the legs are moving. If the posture muscles are weak a runner will lose form towards the end of a race, he will roll from side to side, and less and less of his energy expended will be used in forward movement.

Resistance work in general will have some of the effects of hill running and some of those of cross-country running. If one does interval running over, say, a 600-yd. sand-dune circuit, one therefore combines the benefit of the interval training with extra strengthening of the leg muscles and general strengthening of the musculature. Running in boots has roughly the same effect, and in addition I have found it useful in preventing injuries. The extra support given to the foot by the rigid sole of the boots will often prevent the incidence of strains and bruising which might otherwise result from too much running on hard surfaces.

In spite of these added benefits, I would not advise anyone to do all his running in boots over sand dunes. He would become very strong in this way, but he would not at the same time acquire the heart/lung adaptation to prolonged work at speed, because he would not be running fast enough.

Speed Training

The training we have discussed so far will make a runner strong and fit. Two more things are needed to make him a complete athlete—sprinting speed and race experience. Of the tactical and strategic aspects of racing I shall speak in another chapter, but there is no doubt that there is a marked physical benefit from racing. This can be seen very easily in schoolboy runners, who often do no specific training, but improve through the season purely as a result of racing. This is understandable—after all, the training I have described is all an attempt to simulate the pressures of a race. Provided the athlete has sufficient rest in between, races can do nothing but good. I have little sympathy with the athlete who misses what he considers to be unimportant races in order to train. If he does not enjoy racing, why bother to train at all?

A good many runners do, in fact, race in training. This is a thing to be treated very carefully. If a group of runners is racing in training as well as at week-ends the effects on the weaker members may be more harmful than beneficial. On the other hand, a really fit, mature athlete may find that racing against himself or in his training group at regular intervals gives him very high quality training without imposing any nervous strain.

Pure speed training must have a place in any athlete's programme. Whatever his distance there will come a time, and often it may be in his most important race, when he has to sprint to win; classic examples of this were seen in the Tokyo Olympics, in the finish of the 10,000 metres and the duel for second place in the marathon. The muscular strength may be developed by resistance training or weight training, but the technique of sprinting must be learnt and the habit kept up. It is no good waiting till summer to sharpen up. During the winter training new muscle fibres and sheaths will be formed. If speed training, by which I mean repeated short bursts of 30–100 yds., working up to maximum speed, is carried out regularly through the year, then these newly formed muscles will maintain their flexibility. If the runner does no speed work in winter, he will find that it takes him longer to adjust to faster running in the summer, and stiffness may hinder or completely prevent his training for several days, besides making him more liable to injury.

'Surge running' is one good way of getting through speed work without great mental effort. By this term I mean running at a steady pace, say 80·0–90·0 per lap, if the training is done on a track, and accelerating up to a sprint in each lap. A 440-yd. lap would therefore be made up of 110 yds. running, 30 yds. acceleration, 40 yds. sprinting, 30 yds. deceleration, 110 yds. running, 30 yds. acceleration, 40 yds. sprinting, 30 yds. deceleration and so on. In this way one can get through a useful amount of work, say 20 × 100 yds., in a short time, about 15 min. This can be done after a long run in winter, when one is properly warmed up, or in summer as a prelude to the main session.

Weight Training

I have left weight training and exercises till last since they do not fall so easily into the pattern of discussion. The value of exercising is obvious. The running action involves most muscles in the body, and it is common sense to keep the general muscular system fit and supple. A period of 5–10 min. per day on general exercises, including those for muscle groups in arms, chest, back, stomach, trunk, and legs is time well spent. In particular it is important to strengthen the muscles of the stomach and back, which keep the body rigid while the legs are moving. It is also necessary to have strong arms and shoulders, to counteract the turning effect of the alternate leg movement, particularly pronounced when sprinting. It is here that weight training comes in.

Few people would deny that weight training has a most important place in the training of sprinters; working against weights increases muscle size and strength, and a larger stronger muscle can accelerate the body faster. It follows that this type of training must have a beneficial effect on the sprinting speed of distance runners, and I would not hesitate to recommend weight training to prospective half-mile and mile runners. When one is considering longer distances, however, one has to consider how much time is available and whether this time might not be better spent on running. If the athlete is young, and not definitely committed to an event, he would be well advised to make use of weights where they are available and to develop his capabilities as fully as possible in this direction. If you are a runner training for long distance—3 miles and above—then I would suggest that you do weight training only if you can spare an additional 30 min. a day, twice a week, on top of your running schedule. Weight training, like any other type of training, must be done regularly if it is to have any beneficial effect. I suggest that you stick to a small number of exercises which cover legs, trunk, and upper body muscle groups, and see how far you progress. It is physiologically sounder to do a small number of repetitions with near-maximum poundage to build up the strength in the muscles. The muscles which have to take prolonged use will receive their endurance training in your running.

I have not included any particular instruction on weight training, since there are good books written by experts on the subject.[1] I would, however, remind athletes to learn to

[1] Especially *Strength Training for Athletics*, R. J. Pickering, published by the Amateur Athletic Association.

lift properly before they start using maximum poundages, and to pay attention to the safety precautions.

Isometric training, which means contracting the muscle the maximum amount without performing any movement, is at the time of writing an unproven form of training. It appears to produce a rapid increase in strength in the untrained muscle, but without conferring any powers of endurance. It does, however, help to maintain muscle tone, and it does not require much time or special equipment. It can do no harm and may bring some benefits, particularly to those who do not have facilities available for normal weight training.

Altitude Training

The decision to hold the 1968 Olympic Games in Mexico City at a height of 7400 ft. has had a number of effects on athletics. Not the least of these is the discovery that training at a high altitude has an additional beneficial effect on one's performance at sea level. This has been suspected for some time, for example, in the days of the British Army in India, horses which were trained in the hill stations were not allowed to compete against those in the plains, because they were so much better. Indications relevant to athletics have come from the remarkable world records set up by Kipchoge Keino (7:39 for 3000 metres) and Gaston Roelants (58:06 for 20,000 metres and 12 miles 1478 yds. in one hour) immediately after coming down from training at high altitudes.

The benefit obtained is an improvement in the oxygen transport system, mainly an increase in the quantity of haemoglobin in the blood. It is likely that this factor will have a considerable effect on athletics at international level, giving an advantage to those countries with the facilities and the money to give their athletes this 'booster'. Indeed it has already had an effect. In the 1966 G.B. *v.* U.S.S.R. match we were amazed by the high level of performance of the Soviet distance runners. In the 1500 metres their men improved two or three seconds on their previous best times. In the 3000 metres steeplechase, the 5000 and 10,000 metres our athletes ran in a manner that would have given them victory in most international matches, only to be beaten by superb performances by the Russians. In the 10,000 metres for example, I beat the existing U.K. all-comers record, but still finished third. If the Russian athletes had gone on to win medals in the European Championships of that year none of us would have been surprised but, with the exception of the steeplechase, they did not. In the 1500, 5000, and 10,000 metres none of the Russians who had run so well in June even approached those performances at the end of August, whereas the British athletes, in spite of having just returned from Jamaica, at least put up a reasonable showing (fourth in the 1500 metres, fourth in the 5000 metres, fifth and sixth in the 10,000 metres).

There is no doubt in my mind that the reason for the spectacular performances of the Russian runners was the fact, revealed in conversation after the match, that their distance men had spent nearly four weeks together in a training camp at altitude. It seems certain that this gives an advantage. On the other hand it is expensive, it takes several weeks to obtain the full benefits, and the effects wear off after a week or so. It is to be hoped that these considerations will limit the effects of the altitude factor on international athletics.

6

Planning a Training Schedule

EVERY runner should have a target and a plan to reach it. In a progressive training plan you must start with the possible and move on to the impossible. The first step is to examine carefully your own capabilities and your own weaknesses, for example: do you lack a fast finish? Do you become upset by a fast start? Do you find that you weaken half-way through a race but still have a good bit left at the end? Do you tend to become discouraged by bad conditions? Do you become inhibited by superior opposition? Your training plan must aim to eliminate these weak points. Basically, however, it is concerned with enabling you to run faster for longer than you were capable of the year before.

For most British athletes the winter season is used both for track training and for competition in road or cross-country races. You therefore have to plan your training so as to take account of, and where possible make use of, the races in which you will be taking part.

The general plan is to start with extensive, fairly leisurely work on different factors, and then make the training more intensive as the racing season comes nearer. This is, I believe, an approach which falls in with the natural rhythm of the body's adjustments. It is impossible to maintain a schedule of ferocious intensity, with every session at maximum effort, for any length of time without injury resulting. The pattern should be: (1) Easy work, (2) Build up, (3)

62

Interval work, (4) Short rest, (5) Race, (6) Easy work. This can be the overall pattern for the year's cycle, for each minor cycle within the year, which may be of 4–8 weeks, and for the weekly cycle, which will be necessary if the athlete is running every week-end. The minor cycle of 4–8 weeks is necessary, I feel, for psychological reasons. The normal athlete must have some sort of goal or challenge in the reasonably near future to make his work interesting.

For the first part of the schedule I recommend getting away from the track completely. This period will start directly the competitive track season ends. I see no point in resting completely at this time. If you enjoy running, it is good to run easily in pleasant surroundings for a short time each day; if you wish to explore other forms of exercise, now is the time to do it. Whether it is rock climbing, rowing, table tennis, or squash, it is all useful. The more you can build a platform of all-round toughness, the better you will be placed for the real training. I have no time for the athlete who is always fretting about his health. There is a difference between being sensible and being fussy.

During the first part of the schedule you will not be working very intensively. It is therefore best to avoid racing for the first 3–4 weeks, or, if you do, not to take it too seriously. After this the race can be fitted in and regarded as a hard training session. This does not mean you ease off if it gets tough; in a hard session you must do what you set out to do, if it is physically possible. What is means is that the success is judged not on one single race or one single training session, but a whole programme extending over several weeks. If it has all gone according to plan, good; if you have failed in some respects, then you have something to improve on next time round.

Your training should be harder than it was the previous year; this can be used as a starting point. The safest way

physically is to start by increasing the volume of running—
the total miles or hours per week, up to the amount you have
decided. Once you know that your body can absorb that
volume of running you should start increasing the intensity,
by bringing in *fartlek* runs instead of steady runs, starting
on resistance work, whichever kind suits your particular
situation, and then moving on to interval and repetition
work.

I have discussed in a previous chapter the ways in which
running can be fitted in with your normal life. You should
be able to work out how much time you can spare, and
therefore how much training you can do in each week.
You now have to make a plan on a month by month basis
as to what lines it will take. The best way is to work back-
wards. What were your best racing performances last year?
What are your targets for next season? What speeds will you
hope to be running at in training to achieve these targets?
These questions will help you to decide on the speed of your
intervals and repetition work. If last year you achieved a
4:30 mile then you might fix your target for next season at
4:15. This represents just under 64 sec. per lap. This will
be the speed to aim at in your best short-interval, repetition
or time-trial sessions just before the competitive season. For
specific mile training you will need to run 8–12 × 440 yds.,
or 12–15 × 330, or 3 × 880, or 20 × 220, with as short an
interval as possible. You will also be doing some speed
work, running 100, 220, or 330 yds. at a faster pace with a
longer interval, and some general endurance training. If
you are intending to compete at 880 yds. or 3 miles as well
as a mile you will need to include sessions devoted to these
events as well. You therefore have many possible types of
session to select for your schedule. You might decide on, say,
one short interval session of 15 × 330 yds. with an interval of
75·0, a 'muscle metabolism' session of 4 × 220 repeated three
times, with 60·0 between each 220 and 5 min. between

groups, and a repetition session of 5 × 660 with 5 min. between each one, plus a 'general endurance' session of 4 × ¾-mile untimed on grass.

Over several months, more of your sessions will become specific, replacing the long easy runs and the *fartlek*. In this way you can see that progress is being made. In the two months just before competing you will have a definite programme of activities which is repeated every week or every two weeks. The pattern of this programme will be the same as that for the larger programme: long and easy, stamina work, special endurance work, speed work, rest, race or time-trial and easy running again. If this cycle is run for two weeks at a time, a longer period of hard work can be fitted in. In a weekly cycle, with a race or time-trial on the Saturday, a rest the day before and an easy run the day after, one can at the most fit in one stamina session, two special endurance, and one speed session into the week. On a fortnightly cycle one could theoretically fit in seven days of hard work before easing down at the end of the cycle.

Recording Training

It is almost impossible to see the pattern of your training and racing unless you keep a permanent record of it. I have kept a training diary and a record of my races for over ten years; looking through this I could see at a glance how hard I was training at any time of the year, and how this was reflected in my races. Using an exercise book, one can get all the necessary information on to one line, under the following headings: *Date, Type of Training* (*fartlek*, intervals, road run), *Mileage, Details* (distance, speed, and duration of fast bursts, length of recovery period), *Reaction* (whether hard or easy, note on any injury or ailment), *Going* (note on track surface if applicable), and *Weather*. All these things are necessary; the second column enables one to see the pattern of training just glancing down the page, the frequency of hard and easy days; the last three columns enable you to make accurate comparisons between sessions done at different times. Below are three specimens from my own training diary.

This brings me to the question of how often one should expect to train hard. During the winter months it is possible by varying the types of work to train usefully every day without becoming over-tired or bored, but when one is training specifically for a track event there are several problems; those of fatigue and boredom cannot be separated. Often one feels tired in training because the training is boring rather than for purely physical reasons. The answer lies in planning a schedule which does not put a greater load on the athlete than is necessary in his particular circumstances. Each training session must be done with a purpose. When he has an easy session or a rest day, it should be adhered to, even if he feels like doing more at the time. There must be regular measuring of the athlete's progress to see the results. Everyone will have their own particular test session to tell how they are going. I have always used a road circuit of just over a mile for winter and spring training, since the going underfoot never varies, and one can do the session in wet weather, when it would be less easy to make comparisons for a cross-country or grass course. I have records for the average of six repetitions, four repetitions and for a single lap. In the summer I have used track interval sessions, either a straight 15×440 yds. with a fixed time interval, or the harder 'three fives'. This comprises three groups of 5×440 yds., with a 220 jog in 65·0 between each fast 440, and an extra 440 jog between groups. According to the time of year the average 440 times for each of the three groups might be 66·0, 64·0, and 62·0; 65·0, 63·0, and 61·0; or 64·0, 62·0, and 60·0.

In carrying out the schedule common sense must be used

Extract from Training Diary 1959

Date	Type of Training	Miles	Details	Reaction	Going	Weather
12 April	Easy *fartlek*	3½	Jogging and striding	Stiff	Road	Wet
13 April	Intervals	6½	10 × 440, average 67·3 (70·0)	Tired	Poor track	Breezy
14 April	*Fartlek*	6	12 strides, 20 sprints	O.K.	Grass	Breezy
15 April	Repetition	7	3 × 1 mile road (5-min. rest), 4:30, 4:52 (into wind), 4:37	Tiring	Road	Windy
16 April	Easy run	2	Jogging			
17 April	Easy *fartlek*	2	A few strides	O.K.	Grassy	Good
18 April	Jog and race	8	6 miles in 29:40 (3 miles—14:45)	Good	Track	Strong wind

Total 35

Extracts from Training Diary 1962

Date	Type of Training	Miles	Details	Reaction	Going	Weather
15 April	Long run	$13\frac{1}{2}$	Steady pace mostly	Stiff after race	Road	Windy
16 April			Rest (dinner party)			
17 April	Easy run	$4\frac{1}{2}$	Steady pace, a few strides	Still stiff	Grass	O.K.
18 April	Road run	5	Straight run, quite fast	Stiff	Road	O.K.
19 April	*Fartlek*	4	Jogging and striding	Better	Park	Good
20 April	Intervals	8	10×660 (200-yds. walk), about 69-sec. 440 pace	Sluggish	Grass	Good
21 April	Resistance work	$9\frac{1}{2}$	6×80 yds. hill, 2×900 yds. on gravel, 2:25 and 2:40; $2 \times \frac{3}{4}$-mile circuit, 3:40 and 3:35	Hard work	Park	Good

Total $44\frac{1}{2}$

Extracts from Training Diary 1966

Date	Type of Training	Miles	Details	Reaction	Going	Weather
11 April	Repetition	16	40 min. easy running; 6 × 1 mile, average 4:56 (2·00 rest); 20:00 run back	Good and hard	Golf course	Damp and windy
12 April	a.m. Intervals	8	10 × 220, 31·0 pace (35·0),	Good and hard	Beach	O.K.
	p.m. Run and football	7	6 × 600 on dunes (1:40); 10 × 220, 31–32:0 pace			
13 April	a.m. Jog	2			Cross-country	Cold and windy
	p.m. Long walk/run	12	3 hrs. on Exmoor	Good		
14 April	Road run	7	Brisk pace	Tired	Road	Cold and wet
15 April	Jog	2	Travelling			
16 April	Intervals	8	8 × 880, average 2:16·7 (440 jog, 2:20)	Sluggish	Wet track	Cold and wet
17 April	Road run	19	Steady pace, or 6·00 per mile	Bit stiff	Road	Cold
		Total 81				

and external conditions taken into account. If you are running intervals in a strong wind or on soft going, then you must make allowances. A 72·0 effort may in fact result in a 74·0 440 yds. If you are wearing heavy shoes as well, you may have to allow another 1–2 sec. per 440. All this should be put down in your training diary. Remember that it is not so much the times you achieve as the effort you put in which produces the training effect.

To give a concrete example of training sense, there is no point in setting a session of 15 × 440 yds. for a mile runner just before his races start, even though this may possibly have been a useful stamina session earlier in the year. There is no virtue in doing vast quantities of training close to the racing season, if you are not training for a marathon. On the contrary, it is necessary to reduce the volume of training so that the runner is capable of releasing his energy in the relatively short time of the race.

The fact remains that hard work must be done to get results. At the very least, the runner must be able to train hard on alternate days, or better still, two days out of three. If he cannot, then the hard sessions are too hard for that particular athlete. The hard work can be made easier by not repeating sessions too frequently and by training with other athletes.

This brings me to the question of how to make use of club training nights, or training camps, whether of a week-end or a week or more. It is my view that when you have people to train with you should use the opportunity to do your toughest sessions, but without making it too competitive. You should make a plan to achieve a particular session and help each other to complete it; if you try and run each other into the ground somebody may benefit from it, but the other individuals will not, and there will soon be no group left. It is quite feasible to plan the training of a diverse group so that you can work in the same place at the same time, with the weaker members missing parts of the session, but still contributing and gaining a lot themselves. For example, I have had a lot of help from schoolboys who have trained with me, doing half the distance of my fast bursts; if I was doing 15 × 440 yds. in 66·0 with 60·0 interval, they would do 15 × 220 in 32·0–33·0 with a 90·0 interval, which would be useful half-mile training. A young miler, doing the same session with me, might miss out the fifth, tenth, and fifteenth 440, so that his training then consisted of three groups of 4 × 440 in 66·0, with an extra 2 min. rest between groups, a good session for a miler in the 4:20–4:30 range. There is no doubt that if you are out to extend the limits of what is physically possible then you can go that much closer to the limits when you are training in company. You may have to adapt your own schedule slightly to fit in with other people, but this is all right provided you do not lose sight of your main aims. During this latter period you will probably be competing. It is important that your training should be showing some progression, and so the races should be chosen to fit your training plan, and the schedule arranged around them so as to get the best out of them. In your first few races you should be testing yourself out in various ways. In the case of a school athlete the winter's training and an extra year's growth may have brought so much improvement that your first races will be faster than your previous best performances. In the case of an older athlete this will not be the case, but you will need to compare yourself with the same period last year. You can test yourself for stamina by an over-distance race, for speed by short races, or more subtly, by using your actual racing distance with pace variations. By this I mean that you can experiment with pace, testing your stamina by going off at a pace faster than you think you can manage for the full distance, and seeing how long you can keep it up; for speed you will run the first two-thirds or three-quarters at a speed you find comfortable, and then run the last 220, 440, or 880 flat out, getting someone to time you over this stretch.

This of course can only be done in races where the result is unimportant or where you are running against people you know you can beat. If you are running against good opposition, but still want to test yourself, then go out in front and aim for a personal best time. You may not win, but the experience of running to your limit is, in the last analysis, the best way of extending that limit a little further.

The problem is to decide when a race can be regarded as part of training, in which case it can be thought of as building you up, and when it is a serious race, in which case it may be thought to be 'using up' the energy built up by training. This is largely a psychological problem. A race which is not taken seriously will take less out of the runner, because he will not be prepared to push himself to the physical limit. He will therefore need less time to recover afterwards, and can get more training done, in the week. Since, being a less important race, the athlete will have taken less rest beforehand the race will be more of a hard training session than anything else.

However, since training itself consists of pushing the physical limits a little further, every race is useful training. It depends on the individual how much rest he needs after a race. In the case of an experienced world-class athlete, two or three races a week for several weeks are quite feasible, since he is mentally able to take the strain, and physically able to recover from each race within forty-eight hours. In the case of a young athlete experiencing top-class competition for the first time, one hard race a week may be the limit, and in between those races he should therefore do no serious training at all. It may be extremely difficult for someone who is in the habit of training five times a week to stop hard training during the racing season, but it is often necessary.

When so much is written about the quantity of training

which must be done, to preach a theory of reduction in training may sound old fashioned. There is no doubt in my mind, however, that success in a race very often depends just as much on easing down in the few days beforehand as it does on all the hard work put in during the preceding weeks. The younger athlete must ignore what he has heard about Ron Clarke, Dan Waern, or Gordon Pirie running three or four races a week; the conditions which apply to him are quite different and he must find how much he can take in these conditions.

Planning a schedule must therefore go right through the racing season, taking account of every possible factor. If this is done properly, then the athlete will continue to improve throughout the season; the idea of a 'peak' is an outmoded one, depending only on your mental attitude to races. If you decide that a certain race is the most important in the season, then it will be hard to work up the same excitement about subsequent performances, and your races may suffer. If you can regard each race as a stepping stone to the next, and give yourself enough time to recover after each one, then you can continue to improve. In my own case, in the 1959 season, I was able to improve from a previous best of 13:59 for 3 miles to run 13:45 in May, 13:31 in July, 13:32 in August, and 13:53 for 5000 metres (13:25 for 3 miles) in September, in spite of taking final degree exams in May, all on an average training mileage of 30–35 miles a week.

If one does suffer a period of staleness in the racing season, which may occur as a mental reaction after a series of championship races, then a mental break of one or two weeks, running in different conditions, is a good thing. From my own experience I have found that during two weeks of easy running, without any real quality work, one's physical condition is maintained completely, and the benefit in one's outlook can be enormous.

I want to close this chapter by discussing preparations for one particular race. In general, schedules are planned so that the athlete runs better times throughout the season, but eventually the time will come when it is more important to win a certain race than just to run a personal best, though one hopes that this will happen as well. It is when all your ambitions are focused on a single great effort that a great step forward is possible.

For this occasion, which for most runners will be the national championship, a special plan must be adopted, but the basic cycle can be maintained—easy running, stamina training, special endurance, speed work, easy running, and race. I would suggest that the normal one- or two-week cycle be extended to two or three weeks.

Because the body takes a considerable time to adjust to training, practically nothing you do in this period will directly affect you in the race, as far as physical improvement goes. The idea of the build-up is to prepare you to release all your effort in the 2, 4, 14, or 30 min. of your race, and at the same time to assure yourself beforehand that you are in the best possible physical condition. You must also take account of any differences in routine which the occasion demands, i.e. travelling long distances beforehand, running at an unusual time of day, or running heats and finals close together. On the latter point, it is advisable to make sure that you can take two races close together by running two races in the same afternoon two or three weeks beforehand. They need not be flat out but you need to know that you can do it.

The difference in this special build-up is that although training efforts are hard, they are interspersed with rest days, making sure that the overall effect is one of increasing confidence rather than increasing fatigue. Let us assume that before it starts the athlete has been training hard and racing regularly at least once a week. If we allow two weeks between the last hard run and the championship race, the programme would take the following form:

Day

1. Easy running 30–40 min.
2. Easy running 20–30 min., plus striding and jogging 20–30 min.
3. Interval training (normal session).
4. Repetition training (hard session).
5. Easy *fartlek*.
6. Easy interval session (two-thirds or complete race distance, at race speed).
7. Fast interval session (normal volume, but at a faster tempo throughout, with longer rests if necessary).
8. Easy *fartlek*.
9. Time-trial (half to three-quarters of race distance).
10. 30 min. easy running.
11. Easy interval session (two-thirds of race distance in 220s or 440s at race speed).
12. Rest.
13. Travel to venue. 20 min. jogging and striding.
14. Race.

If a graph could be drawn of the athlete's physical condition over this period, it would dip down after the hard sessions, and climb up again during the easy sessions. Nearer the end of the period the rest periods are longer, and the athlete is only making an effort for a short time in each hard session. His physical condition should reach a crest during the final two days of rest.

Having made this plan you must stick to it. It may not work perfectly but if you have thought it through it will be the most suitable programme for you yourself, in your present state of self-knowledge. You must therefore disregard what others are doing before the race, put your plan to the test, and afterwards consider whether it needs any modification.

7

Training for the Middle Distances

(800 metres—one mile)

WITHIN the last few years the 800 metres has come closer to the sprint events but, although sprinting ability is needed for the event, it will always remain in the middle distance group. In his present state of evolution man cannot run for more than 50 sec. without needing atmospheric oxygen. However fast he runs he will not, within that time, cover 800 metres. Therefore the ability to succeed over this distance and all longer distances will still depend largely on the ability to get oxygen to the muscles. As this is also the area most susceptible to training, the schedules have been designed to improve these factors. In the 800 metres, however, more importance is placed on the ability of the muscles to perform at speed than in the longer events. Ability to perform in conditions of high oxygen debt is also more important here since, although a maximum oxygen debt is aimed at in all distance races, these conditions apply to a larger proportion of the racing distance than they do in longer events.

It is, I feel, significant that more of the top 800 metre runners of recent years have been men who have either been successful over a mile, or used training of the miler's type even if they did not race regularly over the distance. Snell, Ryun, Tummler, Moens, Clough, Matuschewski are a few names that spring to mind to exemplify this.

In setting schedules for younger athletes I have borne in mind the fact that the developing long-distance runner can only run over the half-mile and mile at school and so, although his training in the summer must be geared to these events, it must also give him sufficient training to develop him for running 2, 3, or 6 miles in later years.

Notes on the Schedules

I have gone to some trouble to emphasize the necessity for fitting training to individual needs, looking for variety, and altering training year by year. These schedules are therefore not to be taken as gospel, but rather as examples of what might be done by an actual athlete in this situation. There are several built-in assumptions: (1) The athlete is keen enough to be able to make some time for training five or six days a week. (2) The training is not so hard that the athlete cannot do his normal work for the rest of the day. (3) The training is designed for British conditions, where it is possible, though perhaps not always pleasant, to train out of doors all winter. (4) The athlete is expected to run for his school or club team almost every week.

I know plenty of athletes who do more training than I have suggested and a few talented individuals who get away with less. My schedules do not set impossible demands; they enable a runner to develop steadily from season to season, year to year, and to enjoy himself while he is doing it. Warm-up has not been indicated in the schedules. Where the training is a straight run or a *fartlek* run, the first part of the run will be the warm-up, but where an interval, repetition or time-trial session is shown, 10–20 min. warm-up should be done on the lines indicated in Chapter 11, and 5–10 min. spent in warming-down afterwards, where possible.

Conversions and abbreviations Interval and repetition sessions are denoted by the number of repetitions and then the distance covered in yards, e.g. 8×330. The rest period, in time and distance, is shown in brackets, e.g. (440 jog, $2\frac{1}{2}$ min.).

880 yds./mile Schedule, 17-year-old Schoolboy, Best Times 2:12/4:50 at 16

Winter (*December*)		*Mileage*
Mon.	Lunchtime weight training, 15–20 mins. 4 mile run after school in group, 25 mins. approx.	4
Tues.	1 mile jog, then hard round 2 mile course (timed), total time 20 mins.	3
Wed.	Games afternoon. Run out to wood, $2\frac{1}{2}$ miles, 6×150 yds. uphill (150 jog back). Run back quite hard. Total time 1 hour.	7
Thur.	Lunchtime weight training, 15–20 mins.	
Fri.	3 miles *fartlek* at lunch time, 20 mins.	3
Sat.	Minor cross-country race—$3\frac{1}{2}$ miles, plus 1 mile warm-up and 2 miles afterwards. Total time 55 mins.	$6\frac{1}{2}$
Sun.	Steady run round 10 mile course, 1 hour plus.	10
	Approx. total	$33\frac{1}{2}$

Mon.	Lunchtime weight training, 15–20 mins. 4 mile run after school, 25 mins.	4
Tues.	30 min. running in playing fields, including 16×120 yds. fast stride.	4
Wed.	Games afternoon. Road *fartlek* with group—2 miles easy, then 6×2 min. fast, 2 min. slow, then 2 miles chain running. Total time 1 hour.	8
Thur.	3 miles *fartlek* at lunch time, 20 min.	3
Fri.	Rest.	–
Sat.	Hard cross-country race—4 miles plus $1\frac{1}{2}$ miles warm-up and 1 mile afterwards jogging. Total time 1 hour.	7
Sun.	5 mile run (easy pace) + exercises, 40 mins.	5
	Approx. total	31

Cross-country and road racing provide the basis of Britain's strength in distance running. Here the 1964 Southern Counties' cross-country field are led up the first hill by, *left to right*, Tim Briault, Mel Batty, Bruce Tulloh, and Ray Roseman.

Cross-country is not confined to men. Here Sue Tulloh, the author's wife, fights out the 1964 National Junior Championship with Mary Hodson, who went on to represent Great Britain in the Olympic 800 metres that year.

The beginning and end of 13 years of running. *Above*, Bruce Tulloh with friends in South China Athletic Club after winning the Hong Kong 5000 metres title in 1955. *Below*, Tulloh leads from Tim Johnston and Mike Turner in the 1967 Inter-Counties 6 miles Championship which he won in the Championship Record of 27:42·0.

Road relays provide some of the best winter competition. Tulloh and Gordon Pirie contest a leg of the 1960 London to Brighton National.

Martin Hyman handing over to Bruce Tulloh after building up a 3-min. lead in the 1961 Southern London to Brighton Relay.

The start of the 1959 Nos Galan (through the streets) mile.

'In 1961 I won few races but gained a lot of experience.'

Above, the Inter-Counties 3 miles won by Derek Ibbotson (35).

Opposite, the G.B. *v*. Hungary 5000 metres. Tulloh leads from Gordon Pirie, Sandor Iharos, and the winner, Istvan Rozsavolgyi.

The great middle-distance runner of his time. Peter Snell on his way to a world 880 yds. record of 1 :45·1 at Christchurch, New Zealand, in 1962.

Spring (April)   *Mileage*

Mon.	Cross-country run 6 miles with bursts up hills.	6
Tues.	35 min. running on playing fields including 20 × 100 fast stride working up to sprint (150 yds. jog or walk).	5
Wed.	4 × 700–900 circuit (e.g. perimeter of playing field) untimed (slow lap jog 5–6 min.).	6
Thur.	Rest.	–
Fri.	5 miles easy *fartlek*.	5
Sat.	A.M. 4 mile run. P.M. 2 mile run. 8 × 440 with group. Average 68 (440 jog 2½–3 min.).	11
Sun.	A.M. 3 mile run. 6 × 440 striding on grass and run back, 8 × 150 hill climbs. P.M. Warm-up and 6 × 150 in relay race. 1 mile warm-down.	13
Mon.	Lunchtime weight training.	–
Tues.	5 miles easy *fartlek*.	5
Wed.	3 miles easy, thorough exercise session, 10 × 220 in 30–32 (220 jog, 2 min.).	6
Thur.	Lunchtime 20 min. running on grass, including approx. 12 × 100 fast strides with 150 jog between.	3
Fri.	Rest.	–
Sat.	Race over 880 or mile.	4
Sun.	Steady run 6 miles.	6

Approx. total 70

Competitive Season (May)

Mon.	3 × 700–900 circuit untimed (slow lap jog, 5–6 min.).	5
Tues.	4 mile run.	4
Wed.	Warm-up and exercises. 220 in 28 (440 jog), 440 in 67 (440 jog), 'up and down' session: 660 in 100 (660 jog), 440 in 67 (440 jog), 220 flat out. 1 mile warm-down.	6
Thur.	30 min. easy running on grass, including several 100-yds. strides.	4
Fri.	Rest.	–
Sat.	Race.	4
Sun.	Easy run 4–8 miles depending on previous day's race.	6

Approx. total 29

Explanations of Above Schedule

Winter   This is based on fitting in running with school life. The sessions can all be done in 15–25 min. except for those at week-ends and on Wednesday afternoons. Weight training is included, it must be done regularly and with steady progression to show benefits. This, together with hill running and some long steady runs, longer than he will have done the year before, will develop him in several ways. Heart/lung training is catered for by the road *fartlek* session, which is really interval training, by the 2 mile time-trial, and by the cross-country races themselves. A session of striding on grass is included, so that the developing muscles become accustomed to a reasonably fast tempo and will therefore be better prepared for the faster work in the spring. The easy runs in between should not be disregarded; they are an integral part of the training, allowing for the harder work to be absorbed and the tired muscle to be relaxed.

Spring   This specimen schedule incorporates a week-end of very hard training, such as might be done in a week-end get-together in the Easter holidays. The training either side of it is therefore a little easier. There is more emphasis on race preparation, with interval sessions and some fast work.

Summer   Since the school athlete is often racing twice a week, little hard training is done. The Monday repetition session is done for stamina and the Wednesday 'up-and-down' session is to measure fitness, improve pace judgment and boost confidence. Before a big race this could be replaced by a few quarters at race speed and 2 × 220 fast, all with longish intervals.

Progression   As the athlete gets older he will naturally be able to cope with a greater volume of training. Within the year he can aim to improve the quality of his fast work; the following year he could increase the volume to 40–50 miles a week, as in the next schedule.

880 yds./mile Schedule, 21-year-old Club Athlete, Best Time 1:55/4:14

Winter		*Mileage*
Mon.	6 mile *fartlek* on road, including 8 × 1 min. hard effort (2–3 min. jog). Total time 40 min.	6
Tues.	Hill climbs, 12 × 180 uphill fast (jog down slowly). Time 50 min.	6
Wed.	20 min. weight training, then 3 miles run, alternating 30 sec. fast stride, with 90 sec. jog. Total time 50 min.	5
Thur.	2 miles warm-up, then 'tempo running' 20 × 150 fast strides on road or grass (200 slow jog). Total time 45 min.	6
Fri.	Rest.	–
Sat.	Club cross-country race.	8
Sun.	Long run. 12–15 miles at slow pace, 20 min. weight training. Total time 2 hours approx.	13
	Approx. total	44

Mon.	Bad weather—6 miles straight run. Time 35 min.	6
Tues.	Resistance work. 3 × 700–1000 circuit over soft ground or in boots (5 min. rest). Time 45 min.	5
Wed.	Weight training. Run as previous Wed. but alternating 40 sec. fast 80 sec. slow. Time 50 min.	5
Thur.	3 mile jog, 20 min.	3
Fri.	Rest.	–
Sat.	10 mile road race.	13
Sun.	6 mile easy *fartlek* on grass.	6
	Approx. total	38

Approx. total for 2 weeks, 82 miles

Spring		
Mon.	8 × 1 min. fast on grass (2:30 jog).	6
Tues.	12 × 180 hill climbs (jog down slowly).	6
Wed.	20 min. weight training. Repetition running 4 × 880 (5 min. rest). Start at 2:12 average and work down. Finish with 2 miles jogging, striding, and sprinting.	6

		Mileage
Thur.	Tempo running. 6×220 in 28 (220 jog). 5 min. rest and repeat.	5
Fri.	Rest or jog.	–
Sat.	Road relay race.	6
Sun.	6–8 mile run, followed by 2–3 miles on grass, striding out fast in bursts.	10
Mon.	16×30 sec. fast on grass (1:30 jog).	6
Tues.	*Fartlek* run 8 miles, bursts of 50–300 yds.	8
Wed.	8×440 (440 jog, 2:15). Start at 63 sec. average and work down. 1½–2 miles jogging, striding, and sprinting on grass.	8
Thur.	16×150 fast stride (150 slow jog).	5
Fri.	Rest.	–
Sat.	Club track trial, race over 660 and 1½ miles.	5
Sun.	10–12 mile steady run.	11
	Approx. total	82

Competitive Season

		Mileage
Mon.	Repetition running. 4×880 (5 min. rest).	5
Tues.	8 mile *fartlek* run.	8
Wed.	220 in 30 (220 jog), 440 in 61 (440 jog), 660 in 92 (660 jog), 440 in 61 (440 jog), 220 in 28 (220 jog). Aim at these times.	5
Thur.	16×150 striding (150 jog).	5
Fri.	Rest.	–
Sat.	Club meeting. Run mile, going for best time, plus 440 leg in relay.	5
Sun.	6–8 miles easy running, plus 2–3 miles on grass jogging and striding.	9
Mon.	12×220 in 27–28 (220 jog).	6
Tues.	Jogging and striding on glass 4 miles.	4
Wed.	3×440 in 55–56 (4 min. rest).	4
Thur.	Rest.	–
Fri.	Heats of championship 880.	3
Sat.	Finals.	3
Sun.	6–10 miles easy running.	8
	Approx. total	65

Explanation of Above Schedule

Neither the time involved nor the mileage run in performing these schedules is of very great volume—I am assuming here that the athlete wants to improve on his previous times, but is not intending to leap into international class in one bound. This schedule can obviously be increased in volume and in quality, but this should not be done until the athlete has actually performed the sessions I have suggested and not just once, but in the context of the whole weekly or fortnightly schedule. There is a good deal of interval work, since this makes the best use of time available. Hill work, resistance running, weight training, and long running are all included in the winter schedule to develop different factors; the cycle contains three interval sessions, for cardio-vascular improvement, two races and one straight run, for 'special endurance', one long run for 'general endurance', two weight sessions and one hill session for strength, and one 'tempo' session for speed, while the repetition session (3×700–1000) combines a 'special endurance' and a strengthening effect. Before a major race the hard and easy days alternate, so that the athlete has a chance to recover from the good sessions and build himself up for the big event.

Progression   As I suggested for the previous set of schedules, it is best to increase the quality of the training during the year. Progress in this can be measured at least once a fortnight in the winter and once a week in the spring. The following year the quantity should be increased, working more on the lines of the next two sets of schedules.

Mile Schedule, International-Class Miler,
Best Time 3:58; Target 3:54

Winter		*Mileage*
Mon.	Lunchtime or A.M. 4 miles. P.M. 12 × 300 hill climbs (slow jog down).	10
Tues.	Lunchtime or A.M. 4 miles. P.M. 7 miles on road, alternating 2 min. fast, 2 min. slow, 1 min. fast, 1 min. slow.	11
Wed.	Lunchtime or A.M. 4 miles. P.M. 15 × 440 approx. on grass, not flat out (200 jog).	12
Thur.	Lunchtime or A.M. 4 miles. P.M. warm-up, time-trial round 1½ mile road circuit and warm-down.	8
Fri.	Rest.	—

		Mileage
Sat.	6 mile run, plus 10 × 440 in 68 (220 jog in 75).	
Sun.	2–3 hours running, walking, jogging, striding with group, in different surroundings or 15–20 mile road run.	11 18
Mon.	Lunchtime or A.M. 4 miles. P.M. resistance work, 7 miles in boots, or 15 × 200 through sand or plough.	11
Tues.	Lunchtime or A.M. 4 miles. P.M. 6 miles easy *fartlek* on road.	10
Wed.	Lunchtime or A.M. 4 miles. P.M. repetitions, 4 × 880 approx. on grass, hard effort (5 min. rest).	10
Thur.	Lunchtime or a.m. 4 miles. P.M. tempo running, 20 × 150, at 30 sec. 220 speed (150 slow jog).	10
Fri.	Rest.	–
Sat.	Cross-country or road race. Hard run.	10
Sun.	6 miles easy running, plus 2 miles jogging, striding on track or grass.	8
	Approx. total mileage for 2 weeks	130

Spring

Mon.	8 × 300 hill climb.	5
Tues.	8 miles on grass, jogging, striding, sprinting bursts of 50–150.	8
Wed.	6 × 660 in 93 (3 min. jog).	6
Thur.	4 mile run, then 8 × 220, starting at 30 sec. average and getting faster (220 slow jog).	7
Fri.	Rest.	–
Sat.	10 × 440 in 60–61 (220 jog in 75 sec.).	5
Sun.	12 miles easy running.	12
Mon.	4 × 880 approx. on grass. Hard effort (5 min. rest).	5
Tues.	As previous Tues.	8
Wed.	Long warm-up, time-trial 880 yds., plus 1 × 440 in 55.	4
Thur.	4 miles, jogging and striding.	4
Fri.	Rest.	–
Sat.	Race over 2 miles.	4
Sun.	8 miles steady, 2 miles running and striding on grass.	10
	Approx. total	78

Competitive Season

Mon.	4 × 2 min. on grass, hard (5 min. rest).	4

		Mileage
Tues.	7 miles *fartlek* on grass.	7
Wed.	3 × 660 in 87–89 (3 min.), 15 min. easy jogging, then repeat 3 × 660.	5
Thur.	4 mile run, 16 × 220 in 28 (220 jog in 75).	8
Fri.	Rest.	–
Sat.	Race over 880 yds. or 2 miles, plus 440 yds. in relay.	5
Sun.	5 miles easy running, then 8 × 220 starting at 30 and getting faster (220 slow jog).	8
Mon.	8 × 440 in 58–59 (220 jog in 75).	7
Tues.	5 miles easy running.	5
Wed.	3 × 440 in 56–58 (5 min. rest).	4
Thur.	2–3 miles jog.	3
Fri.	Heats of major championships.	4
Sat.	Races.	6
Sun.	10 miles easy running.	10
	Approx. total	76

Explanation of Above Schedule

Winter   The athlete here is stepping up the volume of his training by doing an extra session four days a week. The benefits of this will be an increase in general endurance. He will be able to recover more quickly from his hard training sessions in the spring and from races in the summer. He will have to adjust himself to this twice-a-day effort before working too hard in the evening sessions; this may take three or four weeks in the autumn. The training itself is of quite a high volume, involving harder versions of the activities prescribed in the two preceding schedules. It is directed towards building mental and physical strength and enabling him to compete in cross-country. The interval, repetition and tempo sessions foreshadow the spring work.

Spring   This is what might be done just before the start of the track season, with tempo work, intervals, repetitions and a time-trial, but still keeping on stamina work (a long run) and the hill session. Speed is developed in the Tuesday sessions and in the interval 220s. The longer interval work is deliberately not very fast so that the short interval is adhered to and the 'cardio-vascular' benefits are obtained. The

4 × 880 repetition session is a tough 'special endurance' one.

Summer   Here the hard interval work alternates with easy days. The athlete will try to improve gradually from the spring to the summer sessions. This schedule is one without any weight training. A lot of top-class milers do use weights and if they were used in this case the weight training would be done twice during the week, instead of the lunchtime runs and possibly on Sunday mornings as well in winter and spring.

800 Metres Schedule, International-Class Runner, Best Time 1:49, Target 1:46

Winter		*Mileage*
Mon.	Timed road run 2–8 mile circuit.	5
Tues.	20–60 min. weight training (progressive resistance exercises). 3–6 miles easy *fartlek*.	5
Wed.	Repetition work, 1 min. fast, 3 min. jog, on cross-country or road. Repeat 4–10 times.	6
Thur.	Hill running 10–20 × 200 yds. uphill (walk back recovery).	6
Fri.	Rest.	–
Sat.	Orienteering competition/cross-country race/long run (10–20 miles).	15
Sun.	2–4 miles easy jog. 20–60 min. weight training (progressive resistance exercises).	3
Mon.	5–10 miles *fartlek*, bursts up hills.	7
Tues.	5 mile road circuit. 20–60 min. weight training.	5
Wed.	Resistance work. Run out to course, 8–20 × 250 approx. on soft earth, sand, snow, or in boots.	6
Thur.	15–30 min. light weight or circuit training or callisthenics. 10–20 × 220 striding. 5–10 × 110 fast striding.	5
Fri.	Rest.	–
Sat.	Club cross-country or road race or time trial on 1 mile circuit.	6
Sun.	As previous Sunday.	10
	Approx. total	79
Spring		
Mon.	15 × 440 in 72–65 (220 jog) or 8 × 880 in 2:20–2:30 (440 jog).	8
Tues.	Weight training and 5 miles *fartlek*.	5

Mileage

Wed. 'Up and down' session. 220, 250, 280, 310, 330, 330, 310, 280, 250, 220 (walk back recovery). Initially at 30 sec. 220 pace, then working down. 6

Thur. Light weight/circuit training. 5 mile jogging and striding on grass, burst of 50–150 yds. 5

Fri. Rest. —

Sat. · Repetition work. 4×660 (5 min. rest), start at 90 secs. average and work down. 5

Sun. Long road run 10–15 mile circuit, steady pace. Weight training. 12

Mon. Hill running 10×200 uphill fast (walk back recovery) and speed work 10×180 fast on grass (walk back recovery). 6

Tues. Weight training. —

Wed. Cross-country or road *fartlek* 6–10 miles, bursts up hills. 8

Thur. Light weight/circuit training. Road run, including 3–5×2 min. fast (2 min. slow), 3–5×30 sec. fast (1 min. slow), 6×60 paces fast (1 min. slow). 7

Fri. Rest. —

Sat. Cross-country/road race/time trial. 8

Sun. Long easy run 6–10 miles (depending on previous day) plus 2 miles jogging and striding on grass. Weight training. 10

Approx. total 80

Competitive Season

Mon. 8×220 in 26–27 sec. (walk 220). 10 min. rest then repeat 8×220. 7

Tues. Weight training. 2 miles jogging. 2

Wed. 'Up and down' session. 220, 250, 280, 310, 330, 330, 310, 280, 250, 220 (walk back recovery). Aim to improve average. Check total time of session. 6

Thur. 2 min. run, hard effort. 4×220, 4×110, 4×220, 4×110 fast striding/sprinting (220 jog between bursts, 5 min. jog between sets), distances only approx. and untimed. 7

Fri. Rest. —

Sat. Race over 880 and 440 or 1 mile. 5

Sun. 5 mile run, 3 miles jogging, striding on grass including 2×1 min. hard effort. 8

Mon. 8–10×440 in 63–59 (220 jog). 7

Tues. Weight training and 3–4 miles easy jogging. 3

Mileage

Wed.	2 × 220 in 26 (5 min. rest). 440 time-trial. Repeat 2 × 220 later.	4
Thur.	4 × 220, 4 × 110, 4 × 220, 4 × 110 as previous Thursday *or* 30 min. jogging before big race.	5
Fri.	Rest.	—
Sat.	Race 880 yds.	3
Sun.	6 miles easy run, 2 miles jogging and striding on grass. 20 min. light weight training.	8

Approx. total 65

Explanation of Above Schedule

Winter   In setting the above schedule I am assuming that the athlete has not done training of this volume before. The winter schedule therefore consists of a steady build-up in quantity of work, which will then gradually approach the quality of the spring schedule. Since the half-miler is unlikely to place much emphasis on racing cross-country there will be less necessity for him to reach a high state of fitness until just before the track season starts.

Spring   This schedule is for a British athlete, lacking the chance of regular indoor competition. This is the time the hard work is being done, but the weather may sometimes prevent the faster work being carried on in decent conditions. The schedule can be divided into two halves—one week speed and strength and the other 'tempo'.

Both schedules contain less 'heart training' sessions than the preceding ones. There is more emphasis on building muscular strength and local muscular endurance. Before the competition starts the athlete must be trained to endure the discomfort of running fast in a condition of high oxygen debt. This is the reason for the repetition sessions.

Competitive season   One interval session a week is kept in to maintain endurance or, more correctly, confidence in endurance. Otherwise the emphasis is placed on 'muscle metabolism'—ability of the muscle to perform at high speed. It should be noted that weight training is maintained during the summer. This will be lighter than in winter, but sufficient to keep up the strength level.

8

Training for Long Distances

THIS chapter embraces a variety of events, from the 3000 metres steeplechase to the marathon. Both the steeplechase and the 3 miles are considered by some to be middle distances, but in my opinion it is impossible to place an artificial division between these events and those of 6 miles and over, since all of them in fact rely on athletes with the same background. Runners of the same physical, psychological, and physiological make-up can perform equally well in all these events, and if they eventually specialize in one of then, then the reasons for doing so are as likely to be due as much to the competitive structure or a coach's influence as to any specific ability for a single event. Furthermore, the limiting factors, and therefore most of the training, are common to all these events, though some may have additional problems which have to be met by special training. The steeplechase falls rather between the mile and the longer distances; in schools where boys will be running the 1000 metres or 2000 metres steeplechase a modified miler's schedule will be necessary; for the full distance a modified distance runner's schedule is required.

With the increasing number of distance-running athletes, a group has developed whose main ambitions do not lie on the track at all, but instead hope for their main success either in cross-country running in the winter, or in road running in the summer. I have therefore suggested a

89

separate summer schedule for these people; the winter programme will be similar to that of the cross-country/track runner. At the moment there is little international competition between 10,000 metres on the track and 42 kilometres on the road (the marathon). Road races in the 10 miles/20 kilometres range attract large entries in Britain; it is to be hoped that international competition over this distance will become a regular feature in the calendar.

The marathon is regarded by some as an entirely separate event, yet we have plenty of examples of runners from the cross-country/track background having a good deal of success without greatly modifying their training. Similarly marathon specialists often manage to be successful at shorter distances; there is clearly no sharp dividing line between what is suitable for marathon training and what is suitable for 3 mile/6 mile/cross-country training, and it is logical to suggest that prospective marathon runners start on the general distance running schedule and graduate to the marathon when they are ready for it.

Notes on the Schedules (see also Chapter 7)
As in the previous chapter, specimen schedules have been prepared based on a 14-day cycle, for the basic conditioning period (winter), pre-competitive season (spring), and, where necessary, racing season. The change-over from winter to spring should take place about one month before the start of the racing season and go on for the first month of that period. In British conditions one would therefore follow this programme in April and May. The racing season schedules are designed in the form of two weeks' preparation for a major race; if we have only one major race in four weeks, then training would follow the lines of the first week's schedule for three weeks and the second part of the schedule in the fourth week.

As our athletes follow the programme during the year

their physical ability will extend, and schedules which were hard will become easy. Provided illness or injury does not interfere, the athlete should make a noticeable improvement every month, that is, with every two turns of the training cycle. I have therefore explained the purpose of the training for each event, and suggested lines of progression for the athlete to follow.

For simplicity the warm-up has not been listed in each day's training, though it is taken into account in calculating the total mileage. Where a straight run or *fartlek* is being done, the first mile or so will form the warm-up, but where intervals, repetitions, or time-trials or races are being done, it is assumed that a warm-up will be done as suggested in Chapter 11.

Schedule for National Class 3 miles/5000 metres Runner, Best Time 13:35 for 3 miles

Winter		*Mileage*
Mon.	Lunchtime, circuit training. P.M. 8 miles in boots, steady pace including 10 × 1 min. fast, 1 min. slow.	8
Tues.	8 mile *fartlek* run.	8
Wed.	Lunchtime, circuit training. P.M. Repetition running 6 × 900 uphill course, timed (slow jog back 4 min.).	9
Thur.	Run out to park (2 miles). 15 × 300 fast stride on grass (150 jog). Run back.	8½
Fri.	Rest.	–
Sat.	Club road race treated as time-trial, hard effort.	10
Sun.	15 miles steady run cross-country.	15
	Approx. total	58½
Mon.	20 × 200 hill climb (slow jog back).	7
Tues.	Lunchtime, circuit training. P.M. 8 mile *fartlek* run.	8
Wed.	2 miles warm-up, time-trial on 3 miles circuit, 2 miles warm-down.	7
Thur.	Rest.	–
Fri.	Jog 3 miles.	3

Mileage

Sat.	Cross-country championship race.	11
Sun.	10–12 miles easy running.	11
	Approx. total	47

Approx. total mileage for 2 weeks, 105 miles

Spring

Mon.	Lunchtime, circuit training. P.M. 8 miles on road, alternating 1 min. fast, 1 min. slow.	8
Tues.	6 miles easy running.	6
Wed.	Lunchtime, circuit training. P.M. 12×600 approx. on grass (300 jog 1:30–2 min.).	8
Thurs.	6 miles striding on grass, including 10×150 fast (150 jog).	6
Fri.	Easy run 5 miles.	5
Sat.	A.M. 15×440 average 65 sec. (220 jog). P.M. 6 miles easy running, with occasional 50–100 sprints.	14
Sun.	A.M. 8 miles *fartlek*, including 6×200 hill climb. P.M. 4 mile run, plus 6×300 in relay flat out (2 min. rest).	19
	Approx. total	66

Mon.	Easy run 6 miles.	6
Tues.	15×300 on grass, untimed (150 jog).	7
Wed.	'Up and down' session, 440 (220 jog), 880 (440 jog), $\frac{3}{4}$-mile (440 walk), $\frac{3}{4}$-mile (440 walk), 880 (440 jog), 440; aim at 66 sec. average per lap.	$6\frac{1}{2}$
Thur.	6 miles striding on grass.	6
Fri.	Rest.	–
Sat.	2 mile track race, hard effort.	6
Sun.	8–10 miles easy cross-country.	9
	Approx. total	$40\frac{1}{2}$

Competitive Season

Mon.	8×880 in 2:12 (440 jog).	8
Tues.	Striding on grass, alternating 100 and 200 fast (equal distance jog).	6
Wed.	4×440 in 66, 4×440 in 64, 4×440 in 62 (220 jog intervals, 440 jog between sets).	7

		Mileage
Thurs.	16 × 220 in 31 (220 jog).	6
Fri.	Rest.	–
Sat.	Race.	6
Sun.	Easy run 10 miles, including faster work if previous race easy.	10
	Approx. total	43
Mon.	15 × 440 average 65 (220 jog in 75 sec.).	8
Tues.	As previous Tuesday.	6
Wed.	10 × 600 on grass (300 jog), or 1½ mile time-trial before big race; aim at 6:40.	7
Thur.	5 miles easy *fartlek*, or rest (before big race).	5
Fri.	Rest.	–
Sat.	Race.	7
Sun.	8 miles easy running.	8
	Approx. total	41

Approx. total for 2 weeks, 84 miles

Explanation of Above Schedule

These schedules require a volume of just over 50 miles training and racing a week. This is a more realistic target than that suggested by some coaches, and is in fact less than that suggested in the last schedule for the top-class miler, because it does not include an extra daily run. It is something which can and has been achieved by many busy, city-dwelling athletes, with many demands on their time. It was on training of no greater volume than this that I achieved times below 13:20 for 3 miles every year from 1960 to 1964 inclusive, as well as fast times for other distances, i.e. a sub-4-min. mile and a sub-28-min. 6 miles in 1962.

Winter Because of the relatively low volume by modern standards, it is most important to balance the ingredients correctly. The schedule includes long running, *fartlek*, hills, speed and resistance work, intervals, repetition running, and time-trials. None of these should be neglected since each performs a necessary function. The long runs can be taken quite easily—it is really time on the feet which is important here. Most of the other sessions demand will-power and drive to have their maximum effect; it is best to go through the cycle quite easily the first time, making sure that you can complete it, then get down to working at it. No session is repeated in the cycle, except the *fartlek* run on Tuesdays, which can be varied anyway, so the runner should come mentally fresh to each activity. There is no weight training, because I am not convinced that the time spent on it brings sufficient benefit to justify its use for a distance runner. In order to maintain all-round fitness in muscle-groups not directly involved in running, without increase in strength, I have suggested circuit training twice a week, but this could be replaced by light weight training, occupying perhaps 20 min. of a lunch hour, if facilities are available.

Spring I have included here a week-end of really hard training, such as might be done in a club 'get-together'. This is designed to bring out the effects of the winter training, and make the athlete realize what he is capable of. The four sessions in two days, totalling 30–35 miles, will probably take a lot out of him, but having got that behind him he should be confident about coping with the track season. There is a large proportion of interval running at this stage; these sessions will combine the effects of the winter training and prepare the athlete for the track season. The 'up and down' session is specifically done for measuring his state of fitness; it should be hard work.

Summer   The emphasis here is on preparing oneself for the race. Obviously the sessions will be hard, and the athlete will show improvement, but they should never take precedence over getting oneself in the right physical and mental condition for the big day. The quantity is designed specially for 3-mile preparation, but occasionally it might be permitted to reduce the volume. It should be noted that practically all the training before the race is done at faster than race speed.

Progression In winter, unless the athlete is intending to move up to a longer distance, I would not recommend any increase in volume during the year, though it could be tried in the following year. Improvement should be in quality, making bursts harder and intervals shorter, but no one session should be so hard as to prevent the next day's session being completed. Harder effort and natural improvement will show up in faster times for the Repetition 900's, and the circuit time-trials. The 'boots' run and the 15-mile run are not designed to be done at maximum effort, but with the same effort the overall times will come down.

In the spring quantity should not be increased, but greater fitness and greater effort will enable the quality of the interval sessions to improve. This can be measured in the interval 440's, the interval 660's and in particular the 'up and down' session which is designed to put the athlete under a severe test. In all these sessions it is essential to stick rigidly to the interval previously decided on if the results are to mean anything.

In the summer it is the races which matter, not the training. If you achieve your targets early on in the season and then decide to go for something better, you may need to do the occasional interval session to prove to yourself that you can manage a faster tempo, but the real work will all be behind you.

Schedule for Club 2/3 Miles Runner, Aged 21,
Best Times 9:25/14:35, Targets 9:00/14:00

Winter		*Mileage*
Mon.	4 × ¾-mile road circuit (5 min. rest).	6
Tues.	6 miles cross-country, easy *fartlek*.	6
Wed.	Jog out to park, 10 × 600 on grass untimed (300 jog).	8
Thur.	6 mile road run, last 2 miles hard.	6
Fri.	Rest.	–

Sat.	Club road race.	8
Sun.	Long easy run 8–10 miles.	9
		—
	Approx. total	43
		—
Mon.	15 × 220 uphill (slow jog down).	6
Tues.	7 miles *fartlek*.	7
Wed.	Twice round 3 mile cross-country circuit, with hard burst up hills.	6
Thur.	6 mile road run, alternating 1 min. fast, 2 min. slow.	6
Fri.	Rest.	–
Sat.	Cross-country race.	8
Sun.	Long run/walk in different surroundings over 20 miles in day.	20
		—
	Approx. total	53
		—

Approx. total for 2 weeks, 95 miles

Spring		*Mileage*
Mon.	8 × 880 average 2:20 (440 jog in 2½–3 min.).	8
Tues.	5 miles easy *fartlek*, 8 × 300 fast stride (300 slow jog).	7
Wed.	10 × 220 in 31–32 (40 sec. jog). 5 min. rest then 10 × 220 again.	7
Thur.	5 miles of jogging, striding, sprinting, bursts of 50–150.	5
Fri.	Rest.	–
Sat.	Race over 880 or mile, plus 8 laps of track, striding straights and jogging bends.	7
Sun.	6 miles cross-country, then 10 × 220 approx., fast stride (220 slow jog).	9
		—
	Approx. total	43
		—
Mon.	10 × 600 on grass, untimed (300 yds. jog); or 15 × 440 in 68–69 (220 jog in 75).	8
Tues.	6 miles easy *fartlek*.	6
Wed.	10 × 440, aim at 65 sec. average (220 jog in 75) or 1 mile at race pace (4:30–4:40) plus 1 × 440, sub-60 sec.	5

Thur.	As previous Thursday, but not maximum effort.	5
Fri.	Rest.	–
Sat.	2 or 3 mile race, hard effort.	6
Sun.	8 miles slow and easy.	8
		Approx. total 38

Approx. total for 2 weeks, 80 miles

Competitive Season

See previous schedule. Aim at same volume and interval, but adapt speed to that of your races (e.g. 8×880 in 2:20, 4×440 in 68, 66, 64).

Explanation of Above Schedule

Winter The reasons behind these activities have been set out for the previous schedule. At this stage in the runner's career development may be taking place very rapidly, and so it is harder to lay down an exact programme. The winter schedule differs from that of the better 3-miler in two major respects. I have put down $4 \times \frac{3}{4}$ miles repetition instead of 6×900 repetition; there is no difference in the purpose of these sessions—it is merely a matter of selecting a course which is convenient, safe, and preferably well lit. The other difference is suggesting a really long outing every other Sunday, which is designed to build up stamina in the young athlete.

Summer The times laid down for the interval sessions are only a guidance; once they have been achieved the athlete should try and improve on them. We must, however, keep the balance of his training, so that he is ready for his races on a Saturday and for the new week's training on a Monday.

Progression Our athlete will obviously work towards the programme set out for the 13:35 3-miler but he should work to improve the *quality* of his training this year, and increase the *quantity* in the following autumn.

Schedule for International Class 6 miles Runner, Best Time 27:50, Target 27:20

Winter		*Mileage*
Mon.	Lunchtime 4 mile run. P.M. 10 mile run, 2 min. fast (2 min. slow) and 1 min. fast (1 min. slow).	14
Tues.	6 × 1 mile circuit, timed (4 min. intervals).	9
Wed.	Lunchtime 4 mile run. P.M. 3 miles cross-country, 8 × 150 hill climbs, 2 × 900 circuit (timed). 3 miles *fartlek*.	14
Thur.	Lunchtime 4 mile run. P.M. 12 × 660 on grass (220 slow jog).	12
Fri.	Jog 3 miles.	3
Sat.	Club road or cross-country race, followed by 3–4 mile *fartlek*.	12
Sun.	20 mile road run, easy pace.	20
	Approx. total	84

Mon.	Lunchtime 4 mile run. P.M. 6 mile run in boots.	10
Tues.	Lunchtime 4 mile run. P.M. 20 × 220 hill climbs.	12
Wed.	Lunchtime 4 mile run. P.M. 6 miles *fartlek*, then 3 miles on grass alternating 150 fast stride, 150 jog.	13
Thur.	5 mile road run fast.	5
Fri.	Rest or jog 3 miles.	3
Sat.	Travelling; 3–4 miles jog on arrival.	4
Sun.	International cross-country race.	10
	Approx. total	57

Approx. total for 2 weeks, 140 miles

Spring		*Mileage*
Mon.	Lunchtime 3 miles jog. P.M. road intervals 10 × 2 min. slow, 5 × 1 min. fast, 1 min. slow, 5 × 30 sec. fast, 30 sec. slow.	13
Tues.	Lunchtime 3 miles easy *fartlek*. P.M. 20 × 200 hill climbs (jog down slowly).	10
Wed.	10 × 880 approx., untimed (2 min. slow jog).	9
Thur.	Lunchtime jog 3 miles. P.M. 6–8 miles continuous run.	10
Fri.	Jog 3 miles.	3
Sat.	Club cross-country race, followed by 3–4 miles *fartlek*.	12

Sun.	15–20 miles steady run.	18
	Approx. total	75
Mon.	8 × ¾-mile circuit on grass, timed (4 min. rest).	10
Tues.	8 miles *fartlek*.	8
Wed.	15–20 × 440 (50 sec. jog) start at 67 sec. average and work down during spring.	9
Thur.	Lunchtime 3 miles jog. P.M. 6 miles on grass, alternate 200 and 100 stride.	9
Fri.	Jog 3 miles.	3
Sat.	10 mile road race.	13
Sun.	8–10 miles easy, then 3–4 miles jogging and striding on grass.	12
	Approx. total	64

Approx. total for 2 weeks, 140 miles

Competitive Season		*Mileage*
Mon.	Lunchtime 3 miles jog. P.M. 8 × ¾-mile on grass.	14
Tues.	Lunchtime 3–4 miles *fartlek*. P.M. 24 × 220 in 30–31 (40 sec. jog).	11
Wed.	10 × 880 (440 jog 2:30), aim at 2:10 average.	9
Thur.	A.M. 3 miles jog. P.M. 7 miles *fartlek*.	10
Fri.	Jog 3 miles.	3
Sat.	3 miles race, aim at 13:30.	7
Sun.	10 mile run, plus 2–3 miles striding on grass.	13
	Approx. total	67
Mon.	15 × 440 average 65 (50 sec. jog).	8
Tues.	6 miles *fartlek* on grass.	6
Wed.	2 × 1 mile 4:30, plus 1 × 440 fast (56–58).	9
Thur.	Rest.	–
Fri.	Jog 3 miles.	3
Sat.	Race.	9
Sun.	A.M. 5 miles easy run. P.M. recreation, e.g. rowing, swimming, tennis.	5
	Approx. total	37

Approx. total for 2 weeks, 100 miles

Explanation of Above Schedule

Winter The top-class 6-miler will almost certainly be a top-class cross-country man as well, therefore his programme must be flexible enough to allow him to race in the winter. With one big race a fortnight he can still manage to get a lot of hard training in, without over-tiring himself, just before races. The 6-miler's main problem is maintaining quite a high constant speed without getting too deeply into oxygen debt; for this reason his schedule contains a lot of long interval running and repetitions, e.g. 10×2 min., 6×1 mile, 12×660. The continuous running, like the interval sessions, will have a heart-training effect. A man who is going to run 25 laps needs to be strong mentally; this strength will be built up by the miles which he puts in, the twice-daily sessions and the 20-mile runs on Sundays. Once he has built himself up to cope with these he should be afraid of nothing. This is the kind of session that might be done by a British runner in February. In November or December he should be able to keep up the 80–90 miles a week schedule without easing up much for races.

Spring The quality of the work has improved here, but the aims are basically the same. Very little track work is included, because I feel that he can run at his race speed away from the track, with more enjoyment.

Summer In the first week there are three hard training days in succession, the Monday and Wednesday sessions being particularly tough. If he has done his winter work thoroughly he should recover by Saturday for his 3-mile race, which is really a time-trial in preparation for his 6 miles the following week. The second week's training is deliberately light. The 6-mile race will demand a lot of mental and physical energy and he will need to come to it with a fresh and optimistic approach.

Progression By the time the athlete has reached this stage he ought to be able to work out his own schedules. If he reaches these targets he must aim higher next year; either increasing the volume of his extra daily session or bringing in new and tougher activities in his evening session.

Schedule for Cross-Country/Road Runner

Winter
Follow the same pattern as the 3 miles and 6 miles schedules already outlined.

Summer   *Mileage*

		Mileage
Mon.	15 × 440 in 70 (220 jog in 70), plus 15 × 220 in 33 (35 sec. jog). If bad weather, 15 × 1 min. fast, 1 min. slow, 15 × 30 sec. fast, 30 sec. slow.	13
Tues.	8 miles cross-country or road *fartlek*, bursts up hills.	8
Wed.	10 miles run, including 4 × 5 min. fast, 5 min. jog.	10
Thur.	6 mile circuit, easy *fartlek*.	6
Fri.	Jog 3 miles.	3
Sat.	6 miles road race; treat as time-trial.	10
Sun.	2 hours continuous running.	18
	Approx. total	68

Mon.	6 × 1½ miles circuit, repetition (5 min. rest).	12
Tues.	5 miles on grass, alternating 150 fast stride, 150 jog.	5
Wed.	Long warm-up, 6 miles circuit fast, just below maximum effort.	9
Thur.	3 miles jog.	3
Fri.	3 miles jog.	3
Sat.	15 miles road race.	17
Sun.	3 miles jog.	3
	Approx. total	52

Approx. total for 2 weeks, 120 miles

Explanation of Above Schedule
Physiologically speaking, the demands on this type of runner are much the same as those for the 6-miler. He will differ probably in having less basic speed and a different mental outlook, preferring unhindered running on the roads

to the tension of the track. His winter and spring programme should combine the same activities as the 6-miler, though he may prefer to do fewer interval sessions and more continuous runs. The repetition 6 × 1 mile stint in the winter I consider to be an important session; it really tests the athlete's fitness and will-power, and tells him whether he is improving.

The summer schedule is probably easier mentally, since there is only one interval session a fortnight, done mainly for measurement purposes. How hard it is physically will depend on the athlete's ability to push himself. In this schedule I have assumed that the 15 miles race is the important one; the preceding 6 miles race should be approached more as a time-trial than as a tactical race; the runner should try and make his own maximum effort over the distance regardless of what the others are doing. After a long race of this type the next day or two should be really easy. If he has run hard, the athlete will be in a poor physical state the following day, and going out and 'bashing it' will do more harm than good. The successful competitor is often the one who knows when to take it easy.

Schedule for Marathon Runner, Best Time 2:30:00, Target 2:20:00

Winter		*Mileage*
First daily session:		
	4 or 5 mile run before breakfast or at lunchtime	
	Monday to Friday.	25
Second daily session:		
Mon.	6 × 1½ mile repetition running (880 jog in 5 min.).	14
Tues.	10 miles run, steady pace or *fartlek*.	10
Wed.	7 miles run in boots.	7
Thur.	8–10 miles (2 × 5 min. fast, 5 min. slow, 5 × 2 min. fast, 2 min. slow).	10
Fri.	Rest.	–
Sat.	Cross-country or road race.	10

		Mileage
Sun.	Long run, at least 15, occasionally 25 miles.	20
	Approx. total	96

Summer
First daily session:

	as in winter.	25

Second daily session:

Mon.	5–10 miles easy running, if hard race on previous Saturday.	7
Tues.	30 × 220 in 33 (35 sec. jog).	9
Wed.	8–10 miles including 4 × 5 min. fast, 5 min. slow.	10
Thur.	8–10 miles *fartlek*, last 2 miles hard effort.	10
Fri.	Rest.	–
Sat.	10 mile road race, or track race followed by 5–6 mile run.	13
Sun.	15 miles at good pace.	15
	Approx. total	89

Mon.	Warm-up and 6 miles circuit time-trial.	8
Tues.	20 × 220 striding or 7 miles easy.	7
Wed.	8 miles circuit at 5:10 per mile.	8
Thur.	Rest.	–
Fri.	Rest.	–
Sat.	Marathon race.	30
Sun.	3 miles jog on grass.	3
	Plus 5 miles each morning Monday to Friday.	25
	Approx. total	81

Approx. total for 2 weeks, 170 miles

Explanation of Above Schedule

The marathon runner's problems are firstly finding the necessary time to train and secondly, preventing boredom. The first can be overcome by fitting in a short run of 4 or 5 miles into the daily routine; this means that the evening training need take only about an hour. Physiologically, his objective is to run as economically as possible at 5-minute mile speed, and to be able to keep pushing himself for up to $2\frac{1}{2}$ hours. Training must have both quality and quantity.

Many marathon runners train only on straight runs. This in my opinion means that, because of laziness or lack of enterprise, they are wasting time and running more risk of boredom.

The winter training includes one session a week in boots mainly to protect the feet, and a repetition session, which both applies pressure and measured improvement. One really long run, involving $2\frac{1}{2}$ hours' continuous running, should be done every two or three weeks, since there is no other way in which the athlete can prepare himself for the particular kind of fatigue experienced in marathon running.

It may be asked why I have put in interval 220 sessions for marathon runners. Why not 330s, 440s, or 110s? I feel that it is not necessary for the marathon man to preserve speed and suppleness so as not to become set in one rhythm from which he cannot change. 220s have been chosen because they require less mental effort, and because doing a session of thirty requires only about 35 min., giving cardio-vascular benefits at the same time. The other endurance factors will be improved in the road training anyway, so that the extra strain of doing 30 × 330 or 30 × 440 would not give much advantage.

There is no evidence that training more than 100 miles a week brings greater rewards. Several top-class marathon men, including Jeff Julian of New Zealand and Aurele Vandendriessche of Belgium, have tried mileages of 200 a week but without success. Probably the fatigue induced by the high mileage brings the risk of injury up to a level where it is not possible to go through a complete training and racing season without trouble.

Schedule for Steeplechaser, Aged 22,
Best Time 9:10, Target 8:55

Winter

Follow the same pattern as that for 2/3 miles schedule, improving on it as necessary. Add 5–10 min. callisthenics per day for leg strength and flexibility.

Summer		*Mileage*
Mon.	8 × 880 in 2:20 (440 jog in 2½ min.).	8
Tues.	5 miles *fartlek*. 2 miles, stride 110 (with hurdles), jog 110.	8
Wed.	12 × 220 in 30 (45 sec. jog). 5–10 min. rest and repeat.	5
Thur.	1 × 1000 metres steeple, hard effort. 3 miles jogging, striding and sprinting.	5
Fri.	Rest or jog.	–
Sat.	Race over 1 mile or 3 miles.	5
Sun.	8–10 miles cross-country *fartlek*, bursts up hills.	9
Mon.	6 × 440 in 63 (220 jog). 10 min. rest and repeat.	5
Tues.	20 × 220 on grass, fast stride (200 yds. jog).	8
Wed.	2 × 880 including jumps (10 min.), 1 × 440, sub-60 sec.	5
Thur.	Warm-up as for race, 6 × 150 fast stride, including 2 hurdles at standard distance apart (86 yds.).	3
Fri.	Rest.	–
Sat.	3000 metres steeplechase.	5
Sun.	Long easy run on soft going.	10
	Approx. total	76

Explanation of Above Schedule

Steeplechase racing makes more varied demands than any other running event. In addition to the normal distance running requirements he must have the flexibility of a hurdler, strength in the joints and ligaments and considerable speed. The need for quick acceleration and change of pace demands much of the ability of a miler. For this reason the schedule includes more speed work than is suggested for 3-milers. The winter training should follow the same lines as that of the other distance runners, except for hurdling and leg strength exercises which should be done regularly. The force imposed on the landing leg in the water jump is considerably greater than that experienced in ordinary running, and therefore needs special training, if injury is to be avoided. An athlete who is naturally strong in the legs may get away without this preparation, but it is stupid to risk throwing away the results of months of hard training through neglect of one factor. Hopping and jumping should be included in the warm-up. Triple jumping will provide an indication of improving mobility both in speed and spring.

9

Racing Strategy and Tactics

'The race is not always to the swift nor the battle to the strong, but that's the way to bet'—Damon Runyon.

ALTHOUGH much is talked about tactics in running, there are in fact very few tactical manoeuvres. The difference between a good and bad tactician lies in their ability to apply their plans under the conditions of stress encountered in a race. Every spectator in the stands may know what so-and-so ought to have done in the third lap of the mile, but put in that position himself, would he have been capable of doing it?

STRATEGY

There are really only two basic strategical positions; either you are 'front runner' or a 'waiter', a positional runner. The category into which you fall will not always be the same—it will depend on the other runners in the race. Where the runners are of roughly equal ability, as is generally the case in a championship field, those runners with the greater basic speed will be waiters and the others front runners. If all the runners were equally fit, then they would approach the finish in an equal state of tiredness; they would still have a little energy in reserve, since the middle portion of any distance race is run in what is almost a 'steady state' where oxygen use equals oxygen intake. In

107

order to tap the last reserves of energy they will need to exert a little more will-power, release a little more adrenalin. If they do this, then it is the one who can sprint the fastest who will win. However, if the race has been run at a very fast pace then there may have been a continuous rise in the oxygen debt throughout, i.e. there will be no 'reserve' of energy. In this case it is not the fastest athlete who will win but the one who slows down least. This man will win because either (*a*) he is the fittest, and has not reached his maximum oxygen debt or (*b*) he has conserved his energy the most successfully during the race, by not running wide or changing his pace or (*c*) because he is mentally the strongest, and can tolerate more discomfort when near the limit of his resources.

This should help runners to understand why the various tactical moves are employed. The front runner is a front runner because he feels that in a slow-run race he is likely to be beaten by faster-finishing men. He therefore must try and break away, making the race so hard that the other athletes reach what they think is their physical limit before the finish and have to let him go. This task is made harder by the fact that there is a significant physical advantage to the 'waiter', in that front runners break the force of any wind there may be and the following runners encounter less air resistance. There is also a mental advantage to the 'waiter' as long as he can stay in contact, in that he doesn't have to worry about the pace. Since front runners are generally un-inhibited about pace this aspect is not important to them, but the wind factor can have a decisive effect.

The front runner must remember that he will only win if he can break away. It is no good running at a steady pace, unless he is considerably superior to the others. He must start fast, and if he does not break away early on, he must be prepared to put in fast bursts right up to his own limit, in order to be successful. He must convince the others that he is the fittest and strongest, so that they will give up the struggle.

A different situation arises when the front runner is easily the best man in the field. In this case he should run at a hard pace, aiming for the best possible time. The strategy of the positional runner is, basically, equally simple. He will try to hang on to the leader, deriving the advantages mentioned, until he can employ his fast finish. However, this position is complicated when there are others around who have the same plans. This is where a third category of runner emerges whom I would call the 'jumper'. This type of athlete is a positional runner by nature, but possibly lacking in absolute sprinting speed. He aims to jump the field by putting in a hard burst somewhere well before the finish, probably after about two-thirds or three-quarters of the distance. He bases his plans on the hope that the front runner is already tired and will be demoralized by his burst, and that the other positional runners will lack either the confidence or the ability to go with him. Once he makes his burst he is a front runner; if he wins among men of roughly equal ability it will be because he is mentally stronger, in that he can drive himself to greater limits than the others in the closing stages of the races.

For the waiter there is one golden rule—never lose contact. He must stay close to the leader all the way conserving his energy as much as possible. When he sprints he must be close enough to the finish to maintain that pace all the way. In a slowly run race he may go from the bell, sprinting the whole of the last 440 yds., in a fast run race he may save his sprint until the last 50 yds. Apart from the advantages of following the leader and being able to watch him, he has the advantage of being able to choose the moment at which to make his final burst. This 'kick' itself has an advantage; due to the effect of surprise he will gain a yard or two over the leader. This advantage must not be thrown away by slowing down; if the burst is maintained all the way to the finish, then the other runners will have to run even faster to close that gap.

These are the strategical principles. When you go into a race you must have a plan, based on your ability and the knowledge you have of your opponents. You must decide what you want to get out of the race. You must ask yourself whether you are running primarily to win, or whether it is more important to ensure a place in the first two or three, in order to be selected for a team. In the latter circumstances you might employ a different plan; for example, if you were running against A, B, and C in a championship race, with the first three being picked for a team, and if A was as good as you, but B and C slightly inferior, then it would be better to set a fast pace, to drop B and C, even though it might give A a chance of beating you. In a championship field you should learn as much as possible about all the runners, and work out what is likely to happen. You can then work your best plan in the situation. If you are expecting a move and are mentally prepared, then you have already gone a long way towards countering it.

In the 1962 European Championships 5000 metres there were eleven other runners in the final, the dominating figure being Bolotnikov of Russia. The others I regarded as dangers were the Poles, Zimny and Bogucsewicz, and Michel Bernard of France, with Jurek of Czechoslovakia as a possibly dangerous outsider. I came up against the Poles a few weeks before the Games in an international match. On that occasion I did most of the leading in order to test their strength; Zimny just beat me, but as I am not a front runner by nature I felt I could beat him in different circumstances. Bernard had a very fast 1500 metres to his credit and was a consistent performer. Bolotnikov had the fastest 5000 metres time, but was likely to be tired after running the 10,000 metres three days earlier. My plans were therefore as follows: (*a*) If Bolotnikov set a fast pace I would just try to

The Agfa tour of New Zealand, 1962. *Above*, Tulloh leads a 5000 metres field from Dave Power (Australia), Neville Scott (New Zealand), Albie Thomas (Australia), and Murray Halberg (New Zealand). *Below*, Halberg setting a New Zealand 2 miles record of 8:33·7 to beat Tulloh, who set a United Kingdom record of 8:33·8 (see pages 8–9).

The 1962 European 5000 meters at Belgrade. *Above*, Bolotnikov (U.S.S.R.) leads from Tulloh in the early stages. *Below*, Tulloh leads at the bell from Zimny and Boguscewicz of Poland and Michel Bernard (France).

Tulloh wins from Zimny, Bolotnikov, and Boguscewicz. His account of this race appears on pages 110–11.

The Tullohs training with Sid and Mary Rand; Clive Tulloh and Alison
Rand are the armchair spectators.

Even when competing and training 12 months in the year, there is time
for relaxation.

Herb Elliott (Australia) winning the 1958 G.B. *v.* Commonwealth 880 yds. Elliott, one of the greatest-ever middle-distance competitors, was never beaten over one mile or 1500 metres.

Michel Jazy (France) narrowly beating Mike Wiggs in the 1960 G.B. *v.* France 1500 metres. Jazy inspired French athletics for a decade and climaxed his career with a fine tactical win in the 1966 European 5000 metres, see pages 120–22.

Speed beats endurance. Jim Ryun (U.S.A.), world record-holder for 880 yds. and one mile, strides away from Kipchoge Keino (Kenya), world record-holder for 3000 metres, in the 1967 Emsley Carr mile (see pages 118–19).

Ron Clarke (Australia), the 'runner's runner', demonstrating his vast superiority over 'ordinary' internationals as he leads the 1966 A.A.A. 3 miles field by the length of the straight.

hang on. (*b*) If Bolotnikov did not get away I would have to watch the others for a break. (*c*) If no one did anything decisive, then I would go myself in the last 800 metres as I did not want to risk all in a last lap sprint.

As it turned out, the third plan worked without the front running expected from Bolotnikov, and nobody else seemed to have much idea of what to do. I took off on the back straight of the eleventh lap and, covering the last 600 metres in 87 sec., won easily from Zimny and Bolotnikov.

A runner in club and school competition may often find himself in a field where there is a great diversity of talent, some much better than him, some much worse, others unknown. In this situation he must run the race that suits him best, i.e. run a a level pace aiming for a personal best performance. If somebody else is running at this pace, then they can help each other along, but he should stick to his own plan as far as possible.

This brings me to the principle I mentioned at the beginning of the chapter, that of sticking to the plan you have made, and applying your strategical principles in the stress of competition. How often we see a front runner going off at a furious pace and then, when he feels tired, dropping to a mere 'doddle' which others can follow without difficulty. How often we see a positional runner allowing himself to be dropped by 30 yds. at the three-quarter distance, and then make up 20 yds. on the last lap, showing that it was lack of confidence, not lack of ability, which lost him the race. How often do we see a group of runners slowing down and bunching up in the later stages of a race and, although they must know that only one of them can win the final sprint, none has the courage to make a break.

The front runner must realize that he is not often going to break the field from the start, and probably not even by the half distance; it is only when he himself is already feeling very tired that the others will be reaching breaking point and this is the time when his greatest mental effort is required.

Similarly the positional runner who wants to win must hang on at all costs, even if he feels that by doing so he runs the risk of not finishing. He must realize that unless he is almost dropping, the front runner is also at a crucial point in the race and may be forced to slow down at any time.

The jumper must remember that his jump will be most successful when others are most unprepared for it, when the race has gone to a point where nobody is still fresh, but has not reached the point where they are prepared to sprint all the way to the finish. He must realize that his jump is a gamble, a bluff, and to be successful it must be convincing; the burst must be maintained until contact has been broken, if it is physically possible.

TACTICS

Apart from these strategical considerations there are several lesser tactical points which the runner can use to his advantage in a race. Many quite intelligent athletes behave stupidly in the excitement of a race; the man who keeps a cool head can often beat opponents who are physically much more able.

Running Wide

This is the most common of faults. A runner who runs in the second lane for a single lap runs 8 yds. extra. This is usually more than the margin between first and second. The energy expended in running those extra 8 yds. can never be regained. If the pace is very slow then covering the longer distance at a slightly faster pace may not increase the oxygen debt, but at the pace of most races of 5000 metres or less it almost certainly will.

Conservation of Energy

Any movement additional to the running action, any sudden acceleration or deceleration, involves a loss of energy, of which you have only a limited amount in a race. Elbowing your opponents, talking, and turning around, are all wasteful and pointless activities. At the start of a race you should get into your running rhythm, get as close to the edge of the kerb as possible and keep out of other people's way. The only exception to this I would accept is when the track is cut up or when there is a danger of being boxed in. The latter point I will discuss later; the former is a valid reason if the inside lane is so cut up as to interfere with the rhythm of your running. Unless it is exceptionally bad I would suggest running close to the kerb on the bends, and moving out to the second lane on the straights.

Level Pace Running

This offers the best way of saving energy. The closer a race is to level pace, the more economical it is of effort. The overall strategic plan may in fact forbid level pace running, but even within a single lap energy can be saved. If a front runner makes a burst and opens a gap, it is more economical to close that gap slowly than to close it quickly. Very often the front runner, having made the burst, slows down to a pace below that at which he was running before, and it is merely necessary to maintain the original pace. If the gap remains open, it is more efficient to close it by running a full quarter mile at, say, 2 secs. faster, than to make up those 2 sec. in 110 yds. You can test this out in training; run a lap in, say, 70 sec. and follow it by a lap in 68 sec. Repeat this after a rest, and in the second quarter run the first 110 yds. in 15·5 sec. instead of 17·5 sec. You will find it much harder to complete this lap in 68, than the first. The change of effort may not be so noticeable in a race, but it is there all the same.

As general strategy, level pace running is only a good thing when you are concerned about the time rather than your finishing position. Running in front at a level pace is just making things easy for your opponents.

Team Running

In many races on and off the track you will find yourself running as a member of a team and you can often help each other along by sharing the pacemaking, thus ensuring that you all put up a fast time, without imposing too much strain on any individual. You must, however, make sure that you are all agreed about when the team running stops and where the fight for individual places starts! Often the points scoring is arranged so that winning the individual race matters more than just placing highly. In this situation it is worth the second or third string in the team sacrificing himself by making the pace fast enough for the first string, who can then conserve his energy for the finish. In other races, especially where there is a large field, it may be more important for the fourth, fifth, or sixth scorer to finish in a high position and it may well be justified in the interests of the team for one of the better runners to run with the back ones in the first part of the race, setting a sensible pace for them and giving them moral assistance. It may lose him one or two places, but if it avoids the loss of ten or twenty places by the last scoring man then it is obviously worthwhile.

Getting 'Boxed In'

Now that races are faster and championship fields smaller this is less of a danger than it used to be, but it can still affect results. It generally happens coming off the bend for the last time in a race, when the third or fourth runner moves up close to the shoulder of the leader, thus preventing the second runner from accelerating to pass the leader. It can be avoided by moving out in the back straight, to the outside of the first lane, and closing up on the man in front. This involves running wide round the last bend, but ensures that anyone waiting to pass you must run even wider.

Nowadays most races finish at the top of the home

straight, giving 100 yds. clear run to the finish. It is usually possible to come through to the front at this stage of the race, if you have the physical ability, and very little extra distance need be run. Often the leaders may run wide coming off the bend, leaving a clear passage on the inside lane.

Let us now see how these considerations apply to the different races, by considering major races of the past few years.

Applied Strategy and Tactics

880 yds./800 metres

At the highest level this race is run so fast that there is very little room for tactical manoeuvre. However, because of its short duration, tactical mistakes can rarely be remedied. Decisions have to be taken and plans put into operation or altered in split seconds. With the race proceeding at 8 yds. a sec., a tenth of a second's hesitation can make the difference between victory and defeat.

In top-class races the first bend is now run in lanes, so that the battle for position is not engaged quite so fiercely, but in many lesser competitions there will still be an ugly rush for positions at the first bend.

The men at the back of the field will be at a disadvantage in that they will almost certainly have to run wide at some stage in order to keep in contact with the leader. On the other hand the first 220 is often run much too fast anyway, and the back runners, having saved their energy better, will be able to come though in the middle of the race, but this can only be decided after the gun goes. Both the front runner and the positional runner must know what pace they should be aiming at, and be able to judge their pace accurately.

The front runner cannot expect to break contact in the first 440, merely to tire his opponents; the crucial area for breaking contact is in the third 220, and this is where he should make his maximum effort. This will also be the most likely part of the race for the jumper to make his move.

For running fast times, a summary of world record performances indicates that the first 440 should be faster than the second, but the differential becomes less the more the record improves. Tactically speaking, a really fast first 440 affects the stamina type of half-miler more than the 440/880 runner because it is closer to the stamina man's limit. The champion of course will be a man who has the basic speed and has built on the necessary endurance. Practically every major 800 metres title of the recent years has gone to the fast-finishing 'waiter'. Nowhere was this better shown than in the women's Olympic final of 1964 when Anne Packer, originally a long jumper/sprinter turned quarter-miler and finally half-miler, thrashed Maryvonne Dupureur and a field of top-class half-milers who were just as fit, but not fast enough. In the Olympic 800 metres of 1960 and 1964 nobody was strong enough to burn off Peter Snell, and in the latter Games he took over as he pleased, demolishing the field when he strode out. In the European Championships of 1962 and 1966, the fast finish of Manfred Matuschewski was too much for any of his opponents; this man was never a dominating figure, in the sense of one who churns out fast times every week-end, but he was a man who could channel his efforts into one explosive burst just when it mattered.

The pattern to be expected in top-class races can be seen in the table below:

Athlete and Race	*1st 200 metres*	*2nd 200 metres*	*3rd 200 metres*	*4th 200 metres*	*Time*
Snell (1960 Olympic 800 metres final)	25·6e	26·6e	27·1e	27·0e =	1:46·3
Snell (1962 800 metres world record)	25·0	25·7e	25·8e	27·8e =	1:44·3
Snell (1964 Olympic 800 metres final)	25·0e	27·2e	27·2e	25·7 =	1:45·1
Ryun (1966 880 yds. world record)	26·2	27·1	26·1	25·5 =	1:44·9

Boulter (1966 G.B. v. U.S.S.R. 800 metrex)	25·5	26·9	27·3	27·8 = 1:47·5
Matuschewski (1966 European 800 metres final)	25·7	26·0	27·8	26·4 = 1:45·9
Nikolic (1966 European women's 800 metres final)	28·9	30·0	31·1	32·8 = 2:02·8

In most of the races listed, each succeeding 200 metres is slower than the one before. The exceptions occur where a fast finisher has produced a kick in the last 200 metres of a championship race; Jim Ryun's world 880 yds. record is unique in this group in having the second lap faster than the first; this indicates to me that Ryun can go faster, when he gets someone to take him through the first lap faster in the right conditions. The front runner's only chance is to keep the pace going in the third section and hope the others give up; this worked for Vera Nikolic in the European 800 metres, but then there was no Anne Packer around.

1500 metres/1 mile

Although times have improved greatly over the past few years, tactical considerations in the mile remain the same. The fascination of the four-lap race lies in the fact that it affords more opportunity for the front runner to break away than in the half-mile, but since the middle period of the race, between the first lap and last lap, is short, compared to the 3 miles, the positional runner appears, at any rate to the spectator, to have more chance of remaining in contact. To elaborate this, if there is a 1 per cent difference in ability between two runners this represents $17\frac{1}{2}$ yds. over a mile or $52\frac{1}{2}$ yds. over 3 miles. If both were running at level pace over a mile, there would be less than 10 yds. between them at the half distance. The following runner would therefore still be 'in contact' with the leader and the psychological battle would still be on. Amongst runners of similar ability the front runner is unlikely to break contact until the third lap.

The crucial part of the race for him is from 2½ laps to 3½ laps; if he can keep the gap open during this period then he has won.

Looking at major championship races we see once again that with more and more runners reaching high levels, it is the 'waiter' who generally wins the race.

In the European 1500 metres in 1966 Norpoth and Tummler ran a superb team race, with the former, already Olympic silver medallist in the 5000 metres, doing most of the work and his younger, faster colleague coming through to get the gold medal. Peter Snell's victories over 1500 metres were generally of the same type, though here we have an example of a complete runner, a man who, like Herb Elliott, was uninhibited in his attitude, not afraid to take the lead and force the pace.

The front runners are not always beaten, though, and at the time of writing we have two great exponents of this in Jim Ryun and Kipchoge Keino. The latter's victory in the 1966 Commonwealth Games was a model race, following the pattern of his victory over May, Odlozil, and Simpson the previous year. Since Keino was doubling in the 3 miles and mile, many of us in Kingston felt that Alan Simpson, with his fighting spirit and considerable basic speed, could beat the Kenyan if he could hold on till the last furlong. Once the race was under way, though, it became evident that Keino was in charge. Taking the lead from the start, his magnificent flowing stride never faltered and after the half-distance he drew further and further away from the field. The lasp lap was practically a lap of honour for Keino; Simpson pulled back about 15 yds., but this only emphasized the success of Keino in imposing his pattern on the race.

Only the following summer we saw Jim Ryun outclass Keino in an equally dramatic fashion, firstly during the U.S.A. *v.* British Commonwealth match in Los Angeles and subsequently in the Emsley Carr Mile in London. In the first race the psychological pressures on both runners were immense. Ryun, world record holder for the mile, had committed himself to breaking the venerable (seven years old) 1500 metres record, set by Herb Elliott in winning the Rome Olympic final. The whole attention of the great American 'Success Society' was focused on him. Keino, although disclaiming any pretensions to be a miler, was then the second fastest man of all time over the distance, and the onus was clearly on him, the 3-miler/miler, to try and burn off the world half-mile/mile record-holder. As in Snell's world mile record, the first lap was curiously lethargic, over 60 sec., but then Keino attacked decisively, pouring on the pace with a second lap in 57·0 followed by a third lap of 57·1. Even a middle 800 metres of this speed had no apparent effect on the easy-striding Kansan. As they came up to the 1200 metres mark he started running as if the first three laps had been a jog. We were watching one of the great break-throughs in middle distance running. The remainder of the field, 4-minute milers all, looked like hacks compared to Jim Ryun that day.

The re-match in London over a mile proved disappointing in terms of time, but it rubbed in Ryun's all-round superiority. Keino this time was content to hang on and to try and outsprint his rival on the last lap. Any hope of this was lost in the first half mile which took 2:03. Ryun took over almost contemptuously, and from the front he just kept on accelerating until Keino, try as he could, could not go any faster.

3 Miles/5000 Metres

While there are fewer men able to dominate a good-class field over a mile, the twelve-lap race offers plenty of opportunity for the front runner to break the opposition and may, I feel, replace the mile as the race for the demonstration of tactical ability. In recent Olympic Games we have seen all the main tactical ploys demonstrated—first the magnificent front running of Zatopek in 1952 and Kuts in 1956, then the 'jumper' tactics of Murray Halberg in 1960 and the positional running of Schul in 1964. The major events of 1966 proved successful for the positional runner; in Kingston, Keino demonstrated his tactical ability by outsprinting Ron Clarke after a race of unparalleled speed; not only was this the first occasion in which two men had beaten 13 min. for 3 miles, but the times in depth prove this to be the greatest 3 miles race yet seen.

I had a privileged view of this; although England had only sent three men for the 3 miles the B.E.C.G. rules permit four men per country per event, and I was the extra man, using the race as a try out for the injured leg which had kept me out of the 6 miles. From the start the pace was terrific. The Australians were running as a team, hoping to set a pace which only Ron Clarke could maintain. The first 880 yds. took only 2:05·5 and the mile came up in 4:15·8 with at least a dozen runners inside 4:19. One by one the pace setters fell away and as Clarke himself went in front the field straggled out behind him. Two miles came up in 8:38, at which point only MacCafferty of Scotland remained with the two stars. Bravely, though, as it turned out, unwisely, he went in front at this point, but was soon forced to give way to Clarke. The latter gave a fine example of a man who must have known that he had little chance of winning still pushing his tactical plan right to the limit, to give himself the best possible chance. If Keino had been at anything less than full fitness then Clarke's plan would have worked. As it was, being equally fit and determined, the faster man won, with a last lap of 56·3 to Clarke's 58·4, but if ever two men deserved gold medals in the same race this was it.

The European 5000 metres of 1966, though not of such ferocious pace throughout, perhaps imposed a greater mental strain, so that the winner needed a greater than usual

share of determination in addition to his speed and his
tactical judgment. It is much harder to change the tempo
from a reasonable pace to a fast one, and finish faster still,
than it is to go off at a fast pace and hang on, gradually
slowing down, then kicking for home. When the pattern
follows the latter course, the positional runner knows that
provided he stays in contact, he has a good chance of
winning, but in the former case, when the front runners are
continually raising the tempo, he must be uncertain about
how much they have left in them. In this case the race was
complicated by the fact that two of the world's fastest
finishers were together, Harold Norpoth, the Tokyo silver
medallist, and Michel Jazy, who on that occasion had
'failed', by finishing fourth. In Tokyo Jazy had kicked first,
with 300 metres to go, but then had faded and been passed
in the last 100 metres. His problem in Budapest was to know
at what point he could kick and be sure of maintaining the
gap between himself and the strong-finishing German. He
had one advantage, however, in having beaten Norpoth in
the 1500 metres final three days before.

In the event the decision was made for him, but the finish
of the race was none the less a prodigious feat; the first ten
laps were run at 67 sec. speed, fairly slow for a championship race, with the whole field bunched. With two and a half
laps to go Kiss of Hungary shot into the front, and the pace
hotted up to 61·7 for the lap, but as the field approached the
bell Norpoth came through even faster, at sub-60 pace.
Jazy went with him and the two drew clear of the field.
This time Jazy was the hunter not the hare; even at that
speed it must have been hard to hang on but at least he had
no tactical problems. The faster the pace, the later you
challenge, and in this case 70 metres from the tape was
quite soon enough. The Frenchman kicked past to finish
10 metres clear, the last lap being a mere 55·5, and the last
200 metres 26·6. At last he had proved himself as a champion

5000 metres runner, though he needed to be a champion half-miler to do it.

6 Miles/10,000 Metres

If the 800 metres is the domain of the positional runner and the 1500 to 5000 metres that of all three types of runner, then in the 10,000 metres the front runner is king. From the time of Kohlemainen, through the pre-war years of Nurmi and the post-war years of Zatopek and then Kuts, the front runner has dominated. But now that more countries are producing long-distance men, competition is closer, and there is less likelihood of one man dominating the field.

In the 1956 Melbourne Olympics the duel between Pirie and Kuts produced one of the greatest races so far seen, with Kuts setting a pace so fast that the time at 5000 metres almost equalled Zatopek's Olympic 5000 metres record of the previous Games. In spite of this Pirie hung on, and the race was only decided in the twenty-first lap when the Russian finally got away. Pirie, having courageously risked everything to try for a gold medal, fell back to eighth but he had come close to scoring one of the greatest upsets of the recent Olympics.

In Rome in 1960 Bolotnikov took over the role of the 'Iron Man' but by now the field was too good to be shaken off. Bolotnikov was intelligent enough to change his plan during the course of the race and slip back into a following position, from which he won with a last lap of 57·0. He was enabled to do this by his flexible training programme, which embodied a lot of speed work as well as long distances.

In 1964 we saw the trend of history fulfilled. Here was a front runner, Ron Clarke, as great as any of his predecessors, who set a pace faster than in any previous Games, yet was followed and outsprinted by two faster-finishing men. To rub in the lesson, Naftali Temu ran away from Clarke in the closing stages of the 1966 Commonwealth 6 miles in spite of a ferocious first half in 13:24, while the European title went to the youthful Jurgen Haase, a 21-year-old with a sub-1:52 800 metres to his credit.

For front runners to win in these circumstances they must be tactically more flexible than before, prepared to put in bursts and maintain them, at any stage of the race, and to gamble everything on breaking contact.

3000 Metres Steeplechase
Because of the extra effort required and because the opportunities for breaking contact are greater than in a normal track race the steeplechase probably offers the front runner the best chance of success. Even here, though, the pattern is changing. The great Gaston Roelants, who had dominated every steeplechase he had appeared in since 1961, employed rather more careful tactics than usual in the Tokyo Olympics, preferring to break away with a very powerful second kilometre rather than risk leading all the way. In the 1966 European Championships he was rash enough to attempt a double by combining his speciality with the 10,000 metres. In spite of failing in the latter event he still went out in the steeplechase determined to run everyone into the ground. This plan was in a way forced upon him by the knowledge that Kudinsky of the Soviet Union possessed fantastic finishing powers.

For most of the way it looked like a repeat of the Tokyo story; after a first kilometre in 2:50·9, Roelants had a lead of 10 metres. At the half-distance he put in a hard burst and at 2000 metres, passed in 5:41·8, he was 30 yds. ahead. With two laps to go, however, it could be seen that he was struggling, while Kudinsky and Kuryan of Russia, running together, were maintaining their rhythm. Even so, the gap behind the leader at the bell was great enough to have ensured victory under normal conditions. In spite of the roars of 'Gaston! Gaston!' the little Belgian was unable to pick up his pace; clearly the memory of his disastrous defeat in the 10,000 metres was weighing upon him. Like wolves after a tired horse the red vests streaked up the back straight; while Roelants jerked himself out of the water jump the Russians came over the top, and the home straight, so often a triumphal parade for Roelants, became a killing ground. Kudinsky's last lap of 62·4, with a final 200 metres of around 30·8, showed that not even the greatest front runner in the world can feel safe for ever.

Cross-country and Road Running

I have included these events under the same heading because they mostly fall into the 5- to 10-mile range for senior athletes. There are of course considerable differences in the approach to the two types of racing, and often a good cross-country runner will only be a mediocre road runner, or vice versa. At the very top though we find that men like Ron Hill, Gerry North, and Mel Batty in Britain have mastered both, showing that it is more a matter of psychological adjustment than physical ability.

In cross-country racing the basic principle is to keep in contact with the leaders, or with that part of the field in which you hope to finish. With uneven going, and often few opportunities for passing, it is difficult to come through the field after a slow start, even though it may be a more economical use of effort. In particular it is extremely hard to judge the pace, since you can only judge by the pace of the other runners, which is probably slower than that of the leaders. A few men, for example, Frank Sando and Martin Hyman, have such a good sense of pace-judgment and such self control that they can run at a steady pace throughout and reach the front in the last couple of miles, but they are very few and far between and in the past few years of the English National Championships all the leading runners have come from those who were in the front bunch after the first mile.

One feature of cross-country running is the very large number of competitors; this invariably means that the first quarter of a mile is run at a furious pace. I have found that it is neither necessary nor advisable to go off at this speed; if you start at a fast stride, not a lot above your average speed for the race, and keep pushing along for the first half-mile, you will pass most of the people who sprinted off at the start. After this initial phase, you must set your sights on the leading bunch and run at their tempo. It is here that team running can help a great deal. Different people find different parts of the course hard and easy, and if you have a team mate to run with you can help each other through the bad patches.

Cross-country is the front runner's paradise. Gaston Roelants is probably the most successful exponent at front running since Zatopek; his list of victories in cross-country races is so impressive that he only makes news when he is beaten. His victories in the International Cross-Country Championships of 1962 and 1967, with second places in 1961 and 1963, two victories and one second in the Sao Paulo road races of 1965 to '67, his Olympic steeplechase title and world records in that event and the 20 kilometres, these are the statistics of his career, but anyone who has seen him running cross-country in Belgium will always think of him as the great front runner, with an irresistible start and a flowing stride which appears to ignore the mud, the hills, and barriers. Here is the prime example of an athlete of great confidence, who thrives on his continued success, and is vulnerable only when this confidence is lacking.

With its constant changes in going and direction, the country affords many opportunities for the front runner to break contact and makes things much harder for the positional runner, who likes to run smoothly and save his energy. There is just one rule for the aspiring cross-country runner and that is 'attack'; he must show from the start that he is afraid of nothing and nobody and will keep on hammering it right to the finish.

Road running is apparently simpler, but allows more tactical subtlety. Because of the smooth going it is more similar to a track race, but the change of gradient and scenery, and the freedom from continual repetition of the same small lap, give more rein to the uninhibited front runner. Because of its length and the smooth going, though, road running gives plenty of opportunities for the 'waiters' and 'jumpers' to exercise their skill. Because of the large numbers and possibly the absence of lap times, road races often start very fast, and there is scope for a man who can stick to level pace to come through the field; if he can reach the leaders after having used his effort more economically, he should be fresher than they, and can use this advantage to make a tactical jump, or save himself for the finish. As there is room to pass and nothing to upset the rhythm it is possible to run one's own race for much of the way.

The crucial points in both types of race are often the hills. The best point to break away from an opponent is coming over the top of the hill. If you can pick up your pace and accelerate away while the others are still plodding up the hill you can open a gap very quickly. For this reason one should also go hard at the hills in training, whether it is a steady run or a *fartlek* session. By keeping to the same striking rate but shortening the stride you can keep the feeling of moving fast, and pick up the pace over the top just by lengthening the stride again.

A point to remember in these races, as opposed to track races, is that gaps can be just as easily closed as they can be opened. Without the stimulus of the crowd and the reminder of the lap times, the leader's concentration can weaken and his pace drop without his noticing it. To this must be added the fact that many people misjudge their strength in these races; a breakaway may be mere bluff, which if it is resisted can in fact produce the opposite effect to that intended, since the man who has put in an unsuccessful burst will often give up hope.

Team Events

Cross-country and road running are often more important as team events and there are a number of things which can be done to improve your team's chances. Most of these apply to the season as a whole rather than individual races.

Managing any kind of team calls for psychological manipulation, to make a bunch of individuals into a unit; in running it is perhaps more difficult because there is no direct physical benefit from being a member of a team; each individual depends on his own efforts. But, as the team depends on the individual's performance, so that team can offer the individual something he would never get by himself. A runner who would never get in the first twenty of a national cross-country race can still get a gold medal if he can help his team to win.

Nobody can make people like each other; people of different ages and backgrounds are not going to become a happy family overnight; there is bound to be rivalry and it may take time for a newcomer to be accepted. With a school or college it will be fairly easy to get them all together for training and to get them wearing the same track suits, but with an open club it is bound to be more difficult.

The first thing is to get them looking like a team, wearing the club vest in races, and the club name or badge on their track suits. They should travel to and from races together, as much as possible, and always warm up as a team before the race. This sort of thing develops the group identity and enables the passing on of traditions and of useful information to new team members. Before a big competition, or before the start of the season, a club week-end is useful; without pushing it, thoughts will naturally centre round the team's performance in coming events, and it will become fixed as a goal in the athlete's mind.

All this must be done subtly, without a lot of obvious flag-waving and drum-beating. Distance runners will resent any attempt to take over their personalities. My advice to the team manager is: Give them a common task and a goal and leave it to them.

Just as the long-distance runner envies the speed of the half-miler, so the middle distance men respect the toughness of the marathon men. These are the runner's runners. Although the long run lacks the glamour and excitement of track running, those who succeed in it are recognized as the greatest of all. Running a long way gives its own satisfaction, in a race or not. One of the most satisfying moments of my own athletic career was passing Graham Taylor, then the A.A.A. marathon champion at 15 miles, in the Finchley 20 and going on to win it.

Marathon

Many distance runners think that they can take up the marathon without realizing that there are quite different limiting factors involved. Although speed during the race will depend on cardio-vascular adaptation, general fatigue of the nerves, muscles, and viscera will often show itself in the later stages. For the runner this may express itself as leg cramp, tendon strain, stomach cramp or, very frequently, a sudden draining of energy. This may be due to depletion of the carbohydrate reserve or to a depletion of adrenalin in the blood which means that the supply of energy from the liver will fall back to a 'normal' level, which is insufficient for the demands of a race. In this situation the athlete is often reduced to a walk. In most athletes without special marathon training this effect shows itself at about 20 miles.

The problem in the marathon is not tactics but pace judgment and will-power. These were the qualities shown by Brian Kilby over the five-year period from 1960 to 1964 when he won five consecutive British titles, the European and Empire Games marathons, and finished fourth in the Tokyo Olympics. Study of the intermediate times in marathons, when these can be reliably established, will show that the race is won not so much by the person who runs fastest as the one who slows down least. The marathon runner must cultivate a sense of pace which will continue to work even when he is very tired, and which will tell him when the field is slowing down and therefore when he ought to make an effort to keep up a faster pace.

The point made in the section on cross-country about closing a gap applies even more strongly here. The marathon man must keep going even when his position seems hopeless. Changes in positions in the last 6 miles are often quite dramatic and an attack of cramp can transform an apparently certain winner into an easy prey for the man behind him.

The marathon is above all a battle of will-power, but the runner must remember that most of the will-power is required in training, to acquire the fitness. Once the race is under way then it is mainly a trial of strength.

More than in any other event marathon men must take into account the external conditions in judging their pace. This applies particularly to hot weather and to high humidity where there is a danger of the body temperature rising to the point of collapse with over exertion. This knowledge is best gained by experience, but a look at the times done by good-class men in different weather conditions can give some idea of how much extra time to allow.

Before the Commonwealth Games marathon in 1966 there was a lot of speculation about the likely effects of the heat and humidity; even though the race was started at 5.30

in the morning most of it was run in temperatures of over 80 degrees. Fortunately none of the gloomier forecasts of heatstroke proved correct, but this was probably because competitors were aware of the dangers. In a very closely fought race Jim Alder and Bill Adcocks, probably capable of 2:15:00 in temperate conditions, finished in 2:22:00. In a small field of seventeen, only ten finished, notable casualties being Brian Kilby and Ron Clarke. It has been suggested that a man of Clarke's size and weight (twelve stones) is at a serious disadvantage compared with a small man like Alder in hot conditions; he would tend to heat up more, and having a lower surface/volume ratio would not be able to lose heat so quickly.

Having pointed out the ways in which the marathon differs from other events, it must be said that the basic tactical rules still apply. If two men come in to the stadium together, the man with the most basic speed will probably win (as happened in the Tokyo Olympics, when Heatley beat Terasawa for the silver medal). There will still therefore be those who want to get out in front and break away, and those who prefer to sit in and let others do the work, but the fact that the drama is played out over 26 miles means that the victory is generally not to the fastest but the fittest.

10

Running in Schools

In my first two years of teaching I was lucky enough to work with a man who was and is a really exceptional coach. A good coach should be judged not by one or two star athletes but by the general level of the athletes he coaches over a number of years. The results which Alan Launder achieved in two different schools over several years, starting on both occasions from scratch, with no particular athletic tradition, were remarkable. Not only did his system produce athletes of national class, but the level of participation and enjoyment throughout the school was extremely high. These results were not achieved by concentrating on one sport to the exclusion of others, for equally good results were achieved in cricket, soccer, basketball, and judo. They were achieved by presenting the sport to the boys in the right way.

There is a lesson to be learned here, because there is still a lot wrong with the teaching of athletics in schools. A lot of children leave school hating running. A lot of adults will tell you how they endured enormously long runs at school. A lot of first-class school athletes give up the sport as soon as they leave. Yet running is the most natural of activities and the competitive instinct is built in. With the right approach running can be enjoyed by the majority rather than the minority of school children.

It is no use approaching school runners in the same way as adults. In the latter case the emphasis is bound to be on training and self-discipline, but with kids it should be presented first of all as a play activity.

Starting with the eleven-year-olds (first formers in British secondary schools) a run is often used to start off a games period. The first few runs are done in groups, covering courses of only a mile or so at an easy pace, with short bursts of fast running. This only takes 10 min., after which they go on to another sport.

After a few weeks they start running short courses, having their times recorded. The courses vary from three-quarters of a mile to a mile and a half, and therefore the running does not take up much of the period, nor is the same course repeated very often. Some are on road, some on paths or fields, or a combination of all three.

The important thing is that everyone has their time recorded, and that they are competing against themselves, not against some impossibly high standard. Times are displayed on boards, and everyone who improves his time has it written up in a different colour of ink. This may seem a petty thing, but it shows the boys that someone notices what they do, even if they are not the best.

Later in the term 'Top Ten' ranking lists are made out for each course for the different year groups. This means that quite a large number of boys are involved since the same ten will not head the list on every course, perhaps twenty or so out of ninety in each year group. Many of the leading names will be the 'naturals'—big, strong, well-developed boys, who will also be in school teams for other sports, but others will be boys who have no ability for ball games, but find they can run. The psychological benefits of achievement, even on a small scale in one sphere of activity, can be considerable. I have heard both parents and teachers comment on how boys have benefited from their success in sport. The old idea that running is bad for people is fast disappearing, and when one looks at the enthusiastic competitors in events like the Waterloo Road Races it is hard to understand how it was ever believed.

The other fallacy which is being disproved is that competition is bad for young runners. We have found that they thrive on it. At this age (under 14) I do not believe in pushing the idea of hard training, but we do give them as much competition as possible—form races, inter-house races, and inter-school races. Much of it is of a fairly low standard, and the courses are short. It is long courses and intense mental pressure that kills enjoyment. Running races is natural. If the younger runners want to do training in their own time they are not discouraged and one sees small groups going out for a couple of miles in the lunch hour. The only organized training is a once-weekly jogging club, in which all age groups are encouraged to join; this session consists of 15–20 min. of slow jogging and its chief value is in the talking which goes on. The older runners pass on their experiences and the youngsters hear for the first time about the various big names, the names of the courses and of rival schools. In this way a tradition is built up and standards are set for the newcomers to emulate.

For the younger boys there is little difference in the pattern from summer to winter. Their weekly programme may consist of a couple of races or time-trials, a jog run, and two sessions of other sports. One way of moving over from the winter to the summer running is to have inter-house relays, with ten- or twelve-a-side, each running 100 yds. at a time in a round-the-field relay. If the relay is run for 15 min. then each boy on the average will have six runs of 15 sec. with about $2\frac{1}{2}$ min. rest between each—quite good speed-training. When the athletics season is in progress, the emphasis is placed on all-round development. They will do many other sports besides athletics, and even when they do athletics they will all do some throwing, some running, and some jumping in the course of the afternoon. Most schools run some sort of standards competition. One which has proved useful is an extension of the Milocarian scheme. This is a national inter-schools competition, based on performances put up in three events by each individual entered. This scheme can be extended throughout a school and used for inter-house competition by the simple method of extending the scale a further twenty points downwards, so that even the least able can score a few points on it. Since it is necessary for performances to be recorded in both track and field, everyone has a go at all events and some may find a talent for some event hitherto undiscovered.

The result of this lack of specialization is that one has a much greater reservoir of talent on which to draw. One does not get soccer, rugger, or cricket players feeling that running is inferior, because they do it themselves and may represent the school at times. One does not put youngsters off cross-country or athletics, because they are encouraged to improve even if they are not very good. You may get late developers coming into running who were useless as first formers; this may of course work the other way, and the boy who was ahead of his age-group at eleven may be only one of many good runners at 13, but if he has not been pushed too hard then he is more likely to keep on than give up.

By following this policy one does not produce as strong a team of athletes as is possible, in the younger age-groups. It is certainly possible to use enthusiasm and apply pressure to young boys, and to make them develop faster by making them train regularly, but this often tends to kill their enthusiasm and when the anti-authority reaction sets in at puberty you may lose them completely. It does enable a lot of kids to enjoy a good sport (and a cheap one) with the result that a lot of them are prepared to give it a go later on in their school life.

In the under-17 age group the better school athletes will be widening their horizons and competing in open youth events, on an area or national basis. It is here that the teacher or coach can help by recommending training. Even at this age there will be many who apparently defy the experts and run brilliantly on little or no training, but this is no excuse for those who have a little ability not trying their best to develop it.

As I have explained in earlier chapters the training has got to be integrated with life; this point must be made at this stage. Many children at this age are worried, consciously or subconsciously, about facing the outside world, in the sense of exams and jobs, and some will take refuge from reality in the dream-world of sport, just as others will immerse themselves in art or music. Although this has some value, it must be kept in proportion and a coach may occasionally have to restrict the amount of training and competition in the boy's overall interests.

If he is competing once a week in inter-school races, with one minor race or form run a week, and one or two sessions of other sports, then training should not be more than two or three sessions a week. The general cycle outlined in Chapter 6 should be used, and account taken of the training benefits of taking part in other sports. If a boy is both talented and mature, then there is a case for developing his talent to the full, especially if he is unlikely to get such good facilities and opportunities after leaving school. By full development I mean working up to five sessions a week and a race, plus additional outings in the morning or at lunch-time. I would not recommend this, however, unless I knew the individual concerned, and knew his full situation at school and at home.

With school athletes of 17 and over, there is a danger of the 'school or club' controversy arising. It has certainly occurred often enough in Britain in the past, and will do so again. There is no reason why it should occur, though, provided each group is aware of its own area of responsibility.

The school is trying to help the boy to develop all his attributes as far as possible. In terms of economic importance the academic side may be stressed, and some parents and teachers seem to feel that passing exams is all that matters; he must also develop his artistic, physical, and moral attributes. In the latter respect senior members of a school are expected to show responsibility for the affairs of their school. Translated into terms of athletic affairs, this does not mean that they have to turn out for every major and minor school or house race, but it does mean that where some function or event is considered important by the school, as a significant part in the life of the school community, then everyone who is needed should take part.

The successful athlete will probably be an important member of the school community, the example he sets is likely to be all the more important, since younger boys will copy his attitude.

The athletic club is a free association of individuals designed to give those individuals as much chance as possible of developing their ability in this particular sphere. Here again responsibility builds up between members of the groups, to support each other's efforts. A good athletic club can offer a schoolboy athlete far more chance of development and experience than the school can. The school must realize this, and encourage his participation on a wider scale. Sport in this case is providing a useful bridge of communication to the adult world in which the boy will eventually become integrated. If the school, in the shape of headmaster or P.E. master, prevents this bridge from being established, he can do a lot of harm. It is often hard enough for a 17-year-old who could be earning quite a lot of money to stay on under school discipline all day, not to mention homework in the evening. At the week-ends he likes to be his own master; if he wants to run for his local athletic club then it is to be encouraged.

In practical terms the solution is for the school to provide all the competition up to 16 years of age, but to encourage the youngsters to meet and run with the local club. If there is a flourishing local club, then they can provide the competition for the over-16s, with the proviso that the school takes priority for its own championships, district, county and national schools events. The ideal club will have a group of good runners in each of the local schools; these boys will compete against each other in mid-week inter-school fixtures, and with each other in their club team or their county schools team at week-ends.

There will still be clashes of interests, but they can be worked out provided that the long-term interest of the individual is taken as the main criterion. Where the right spirit exists, both club and school can help each other not only in sharing facilities but in stimulating both friendly rivalry and comradeship among young athletes.

11

Athletic Problems

THERE are a number of questions which are of great importance to the serious athlete and which might have been included in my introductory chapters, such as problems caused by injury or illness, amount of competition, and staleness. I have deliberately left these until after the chapters on training and racing, so that we should all be speaking the same language.

It often appears to the outsider that the serious athlete, far from being fitter than his unathletic friends, is much more fragile. We are constantly hearing that so-and-so has got tendon trouble, pulled a hamstring, or something similar. This is partly because even a very minor trouble, which does not prevent anyone leading a normal life, may limit a runner from producing his best performance, but also because many athletes run themselves into injury trouble with sickening regularity. Some are hypochondriacs, which is not surprising, since the majority of athletes are rather self-centred; they collect injuries and mysterious ailments the way other people collect stamps. Others have genuine injury trouble; where this occurs regularly one must look for some basic fault in the training programme.

The best way of staying out of trouble is by keeping three basic rules: (1) Always warm up properly, (2) Don't make sudden changes in your training programme, and (3) Don't train hard when you are stiff or tired from the previous day.

Warming-up: Avoidance of Injuries

The amount of warming-up will depend on what you are going to do. The faster you are going to run the more warming-up you will need. It should be never less than 10 min., and before a big race I would advise 30 min.

The warm-up does three things: firstly, it warms and stretches the muscle fibres gently, so that they will be able to contract or expand quickly without risk of tearing; secondly, it causes the heartbeat to increase, and the blood supply to the digestive system to be reduced, so that more blood is available to the working muscles; thirdly, it prepares the athlete psychologically for the race ahead, so that he is prepared to push himself to the limit. In warm weather the first reason does not apply, but one should still warm-up in the same way, for the other two reasons.

My own warm-up pattern is as follows:

(1) 5–10 min. easy jogging with track suit on if it is cold.
(2) 5 min. of easy striding, alternating 50–80 yds. strides with easy jogging.
(3) 5 min. of general loosening and stretching exercises for the whole body, including arms, shoulders, trunk, abdominal and leg muscles.
(4) Several fast strides of 100 yds., working up to almost maximum speed, with a slow jog or walk in between.
(5) With track suit on, spend last 5–10 min. before the race keeping warm and as relaxed as possible.

Before a training session I would only include items (1), (2), and (3), omitting the latter if time is short. If one is doing a continuous run, then the first mile or so can be treated as the warm-up. Before a big race it is very useful to have an established warm-up programme. If you are feeling scared stiff it is a great help to have a routine you can go through without having to worry whether you are doing the right thing.

The second basic rule is often broken through over-enthusiasm. On the first fine week-end of spring the athlete heads for the track, puts his spikes on and starts running fast quarter-miles. In the autumn, an athlete may decide to have a big build-up programme for the cross-country season and start doing 15 miles a day on the roads. In either of these cases, the unaccustomed strain on the calf muscles, the Achilles tendons or the feet may cause an injury. The solution is quite simple; you must graduate gently from one type of training to the other. In the schedules I have given this is allowed for. Track sessions come in gradually in the spring—first once a fortnight, then once a week, and since some quality work is done during the winter there is no sudden change. In the same way, some long, steady running is done all through the summer and even in the winter, road-running is not done on more than two consecutive nights.

The third rule is a little more difficult to apply, since it requires judgment. Obviously there will be many occasions when you will be a little tired after the previous day's training. This tiredness should disappear during your warm-up. If it does not, and if you are finding it a real struggle to complete the session, then it is better to cut it down in speed or quantity than to run yourself into complete exhaustion. Stiffness is usually due to over-exertion; you should take this as a warning, and run easily until it has gone. Hard training when you are stiff could easily lead to a muscle pull.

Apart from these basic principles, the chances of injury can be reduced by wearing the right clothing. It is not going to make you fitter going out running in just singlet and shorts on a cold wet day, it is much more likely that you will get a cold. If the weather is really bad and you cannot train at any other time, you should warm-up wearing plenty of protective clothing, e.g. full track suit and anorak, then take it off and do a fast continuous run, coming straight in for a bath and change. Hanging around in wet clothing during or after training can lower your body temperature quite quickly, lowering your resistance to infection, but as long as you are moving briskly, the heat of your own movement will keep the body temperature up.

You should make sure that you have the right shoes for each kind of training. On roads you need a thick-soled training shoe, or plimsolls with an extra in-sole and a thick pair of socks. Running cross-country or on grass you will need rubber studs or spikes. On a firm dry track or field you can use almost anything or no shoes at all. Provided that the shoe fits well and grips the ground properly, the most important consideration for a racing shoe is lightness. For a training shoe protection of the feet is the most important factor.

If in spite of these precautions you still get an injury what should you do?

With most injuries it is possible to take gentle exercise, walking or jogging, without increasing the pain or aggravating the injury, and I would recommend this whenever possible. If you rest completely, then the muscle may tighten up as it heals, and may tear again when you start training. Light jogging will improve the blood circulation in the muscles, helping to clear away unwanted tissues and build up new ones.

This does not mean that you should ignore an injury. The first thing is to find out what the cause is. If it is a slight strain of the foot, ankle, or Achilles tendon, then by wearing heavier shoes and avoiding hard and bumpy ground you may be able to do useful training, but you should avoid racing until it clears up. If pain persists for more than a week, it is possible that you may have a slight bone fracture; in this case I would recommend complete rest, starting slow jogging on medical advice. When an injury persists it is better to go to a doctor, have an X-ray if necessary, and follow the doctor's advice, rather than to press on in a spirit of blind optimism and ignorance.

I can think of several very promising runners who, because they were not prepared to give up a few weeks to cure an injury, have now saddled themselves with persistent trouble, which may in fact prevent them from ever training hard and long enough to teach international standard.

The chronic trouble of the road runner is 'shin-soreness' or 'shin splints'. You may often get this after a hard road race, especially where there is a lot of downhill running, but it will normally clear up after a couple of days' jogging. Once again it is advisable to wear thick-soled shoes and to stick to soft ground. If you start hard road work before it has cleared up it may become a chronic complaint and keep you out of races or you may end up with stress fractures of the tibia and be out for quite a time. Therefore, protect your feet, and don't run on the road all the time.

Staleness

Probably the greatest affliction of athletes is that mysterious disease known as 'staleness', which can be interpreted as 'running badly for no apparent reason'. If an athlete offers as an excuse the statement that he is getting stale, the coach must first of all probe to see if this is an excuse for something else. Was he, for example, still seeing his girl friend home at 4 a.m. on Saturday morning? Was he persuaded to have a second helping of steak and kidney pudding two hours before the race? Could his failure be due to too long a journey or too short a warm-up.?

If there is no obvious reason for a bad run, the next thing is to look at the athlete's training programme. If his training performances have been falling off or if he has been finding it a struggle, then it is possible that he is suffering from a deficiency in his diet (unlikely), or from some mental strain, such as overwork. The latter cause may not be easily remedied, but at least it will provide an explanation. If a mineral or vitamin deficiency is suspected, then it might be worth giving the athlete a month's course of vitamin pills, and seeing if this restores his training and racing performance to its previous level.

If the athlete is performing well in training but poorly in racing, then we probably have a genuine case of staleness. The athlete is fit enough, but the mental drive necessary to produce a good performance is lacking. The subconscious is rebelling against the continuous exertion of the will, which is exposing the person to too much discomfort.

Putting it another way, people are naturally lazy, and if the incentive falls away then the person cannot produce the effort. He may say to himself that he ought to win, that he wants to do well, but if his springs of motivation have dried up then there is not much he can do about it.

The things which cause staleness are boredom with monotonous training, and over-racing. The latter will often affect young athletes who are called upon to represent house, school, club, and county week in and week out. The enjoyment of running can be hammered out of him, so that finally he says to himself, as does Allan Sillitoe's character in that excellent story *The Loneliness of the Long Distance Runner*: 'Why should I go through all this just to give other people pleasure?'

If your year and your seasons are planned out sensibly, then you will never get stale, because the training will not be monotonous, and you will always have targets ahead of you to work for. If there comes a time, however, when you feel you are making no progress, and getting fed up with it all, then get away from running. Ken Norris once gave me his advice on this, which was to get away from running for one week-end a month and one week in three months. This is a very sound bit of advice. Roger Bannister describes in his book *First Four Minutes* how he was doing a lot of interval training and getting nowhere, so he went off up to Scotland for a few days and forgot completely about track running. When he came back the former tensions and inhibitions had disappeared, and his training went better than ever.

Not everybody can try this remedy. In the short term probably the best thing a coach can do is give the athlete a real talking to, tell him he is a selfish, lazy no-hoper. This will make the athlete so mad that he will run a fast time in sheer rage.

On the other hand this will only work once, and there is always the danger that the runner may believe it and resign! The best remedies for staleness are rest and variety.

The Athlete's Philosophy

This brings me to my last subject, the athlete's philosophy, which is of course closely tied up with my first, the athlete's motivation. Whatever made you become a runner in the first place, your motives and indeed your own character will change as you go along. You will start off as a relative 'scrubber' not expecting to win the races. As time goes on you will find yourself among the leaders in your group, accepting the responsibility of being a team scorer. With any luck you will win club or school championships and go on to county and national level. This success is bound to change your attitudes to the sport and towards other athletes. You must learn to accept success without becoming conceited, and responsibility without becoming domineering. One thing is certain—you cannot win them all. However good you are, there will come a time when you get fairly beaten and have to resign yourself to it. This can be very hard to do, especially when you have become used to winning. Any runner worthy of the name will have an optimistic outlook. He will approach his training and his racing confidently, knowing that he will improve. When it comes to big competition, he must convince himself that he is going to do well.

However, any attitude which completely ignores the possibility of failure is not praiseworthy; it is rather immature. In the same way that someone who conquers his fear is braver than someone who has no fear at all, the man who is aware of his own weaknesses and learns to overcome them is likely to be the better athlete. I have got no time for the 'Superman' complex which some athletes affect. One comes across this particularly with young athletes who are ahead of their age group, and win a lot of races. They are apparently rarely satisfied with the races they win, and if they don't win, will produce a variety of excuses. It is certainly a good thing to set your standards high, and to do everything you can to win, but to be arrogant in victory implies disdain for your fellow athletes and is foreign to the spirit of athletics. When you are beaten, keep the excuses to yourself, look for the reasons for your failure, if it is a failure, and prepare yourself for the next race.

You may not have the natural gifts to reach a high level, but you can improve and achieve something by your own standards. Always remember that basically it is not how fast you can run that matters, but the kind of person you have become as a result of your efforts.

In the international sphere, it is very easy for an athlete to be affected by what the press say about him. If he believes all the praise when they build him up, then he will feel it more when they knock him down. You must form your own standards, and judge yourself only by those, and the people whose judgment you respect. If you keep to these standards and put the most you can into your athletics, then apart from any trophies you may win you will finish your career with some good memories, a lot of friends, and, I hope, a satisfied mind.

APPENDIX

Time	Name	Date
1:53·4	Charles Kilpatrick (U.S.A.)	21 Sept. 1895
1:52·8	Emilio Lunghi (Italy)	15 Sept. 1909
1:52·5	Ted Meredith (U.S.A.)	9 July 1912
1:52·2	Meredith	13 May 1916
1:51·6	Otto Peltzer (Germany)	3 July 1926
1:50·9	Ben Eastman (U.S.A.)	4 June 1932
1:49·8	Eastman	16 June 1934
1:49·6	Elroy Robinson (U.S.A.)	11 July 1937
1:49·2	Sydney Wooderson (G.B.)	20 Aug. 1938
1:49·2	Mal Whitfield (U.S.A.)	19 Aug. 1950
1:48·6	Whitfield	17 July 1953
1:48·6	Gunnar Nielsen (Denmark)	30 Sept. 1954
1:47·5	Lon Spurrier (U.S.A.)	26 Mar. 1955
1:46·8	Tom Courtney (U.S.A.)	24 May 1957
1:45·1	Peter Snell (New Zealand)	3 Feb. 1962
1:44·9	Jim Ryun (U.S.A.)	10 June 1966

WORLD RECORD PROGRESSION—1 MILE

Time	Name	Date
4:17·8	Thomas Conneff (Ireland/U.S.A.)	26 Aug. 1893
4:17·0	Fred Bacon (G.B.)	6 July 1895
4:15·6	Conneff	30 Aug. 1895
4:15·4	John Paul Jones (U.S.A.)	27 May 1911
4:14·4	Jones	31 May 1913
4:12·6	Norman Taber (U.S.A.)	16 July 1915
4:10·4	Paavo Nurmi (Finland)	23 Aug. 1923
4:09·2	Jules Ladoumegue (France)	4 Oct. 1931
4:07·6	Jack Lovelock (New Zealand)	15 July 1933
4:06·7	Glenn Cunningham (U.S.A.)	16 June 1934

4:06·4	Sydney Wooderson (G.B.)	28 Aug. 1937
4:06·1	Gunder Hägg (Sweden)	1 July 1942
4:04·6	Hägg	4 Sept. 1942
4:02·6	Arne Andersson (Sweden)	1 July 1943
4:01·6	Andersson	18 July 1844
4:01·3	Hägg	17 July 1945
3:59·4	Roger Bannister (G.B.)	6 May 1954
3:57·9	John Landy (Australia)	21 June 1954
3:57·2	Derek Ibbotson (G.B.)	19 July 1957
3:54·5	Herb Elliott (Australia)	6 Aug. 1958
3:54·4	Peter Snell (New Zealand)	27 Jan. 1962
3:54·1	Snell	17 Nov. 1964
3:53·6	Michel Jazy (France)	9 June 1965
3:51·3	Jim Ryun (U.S.A.)	17 July 1966
3:51·1	Ryun	23 June 1967

WORLD RECORD PROGRESSION—5000 METRES

Time	Name	Date
15:20·0	Charles Bennett (G.B.)	1900
15:13·5	John Svanberg (Sweden)	8 Aug. 1907
15:01·2	A. J. Robertson (G.B.)	1908
14:36·6	Hannes Kolehmainen (Finland)	10 July 1912
14:35·3	Paavo Nurmi (Finland)	12 Sept. 1922
14:28·2	Nurmi	19 June 1924
14:16·9	Lauri Lehtinen (Finland)	19 June 1932
14:08·8	Taisto Mäki (Finland)	16 June 1939
13:58·2	Gunder Hägg (Sweden)	20 Sept. 1942
13:57·2	Emil Zatopek (Czechoslovakia)	30 May 1954
13:56·6	Vladimir Kuts (U.S.S.R.)	29 Aug. 1954
13:51·6	Chris Chataway (G.B.)	13 Oct. 1954
13:51·2	Kuts	23 Oct. 1954
13:50·8	Sandor Iharos (Hungary)	10 Sept. 1955
13:46·8	Kuts	18 Sept. 1955
13:40·6	Iharos	23 Oct. 1955
13:36·8	Gordon Pirie (G.B.)	19 June 1956
13:35·0	Kuts	13 Oct. 1957
13:34·8	Ron Clarke (Australia)	16 Jan. 1965
13:33·6	Clarke	1 Feb. 1965
13:25·8	Clarke	4 June 1965
13:24·2	Kipchoge Keino (Kenya)	30 Nov. 1965
13:16·6	Clarke	5 July 1966

WORLD RECORD PROGRESSION—10,000 METRES

Time	Name	Date
31:02·4	Alf Shrubb (G.B.)	5 Nov. 1904
30:58·8	Jean Bouin (France)	16 Nov. 1911
30:40·2	Paavo Nurmi (Finland)	22 June 1921
30:35·4	Ville Ritola (Finland)	25 May 1924
30:23·2	Ritola	6 July 1924
30·06:1	Nurmi	31 Aug. 1924
30:05·5	Ilmari Salminen (Finland)	18 July 1937
30:02·0	Taisto Mäki (Finland)	29 Sept. 1938
29:52·6	Mäki	17 Sept. 1939
29:35·4	Viljo Heino (Finland)	25 Aug. 1944
29:28·2	Emil Zatopek (Czechoslovakia)	11 June 1949
29:27·2	Heino	1 Sept. 1949
29:21·2	Zatopek	22 Oct. 1949
29:02·6	Zatopek	4 Aug. 1950
29:01·6	Zatopek	1 Nov. 1953
28:54·2	Zatopek	1 June 1954
28:42·8	Sandor Iharos (Hungary)	15 July 1956
28:30·4	Vladimir Kuts (U.S.S.R.)	11 Sept. 1956
28:18·8	Pyotr Bolotnikov (U.S.S.R.)	15 Oct. 1960
28:18·2	Bolotnikov	11 Aug. 1962
28:15·6	Ron Clarke (Australia)	18 Dec. 1963
27:39·4	Clarke	14 July 1965

WORLD RECORD PROGRESSION—3000 METRES STEEPLECHASE

Time	Name	Date
9:33·4	Paul Bontemps (France)	1924
9:21·8	Toivo Loukola (Finland)	4 Aug. 1928
9:08·4	George Lermond (U.S.A.)	18 June 1932
9:08·2	Harold Manning (U.S.A.)	12 July 1936
9:03·8	Volmari Iso-Hollo (Finland)	8 Aug. 1936
9:03·4	Erik Elmsäter (Sweden)	22 Aug. 1943
8:59·6	Elmsäter	4 Aug. 1944
8:49·8	Vladimir Kazantsev (U.S.S.R.)	10 July 1951
8:48·6	Kazantsev	12 June 1952
8:45·4	Horace Ashenfelter (U.S.A.)	25 July 1952
8:44·4	Olavi Rinteenpaa (Finland)	2 July 1953
8:41·2	Jerzy Chromik (Poland)	31 Aug. 1955

8:40·2	Chromik	11 Sept. 1955
8:39·8	Semyon Rzhishchin (U.S.S.R.)	14 Aug. 1956
8:35·6	Sandor Rozsnyoi (Hungary)	16 Sept. 1956
8:35·6	Rzhishchin	21 July 1958
8:32·0	Chromik	2 Aug. 1958
8:31·3	Zdzislaw Kryzszkowiak (Poland)	26 June 1960
8:31·2	Grigoriy Taran (U.S.S.R.)	28 May 1961
8:30·4	Krzyszkowiak	10 Aug. 1961
8:29·6	Gaston Roelants (Belgium)	7 Sept. 1963
8:26·4	Roelants	7 Aug. 1965